CHILDREN TALK ABOUT BOOKS:
SEEING THEMSELVES AS READERS

Open University Press

English, Language, and Education series

General Editor: Anthony Adams

Lecturer in Education, University of Cambridge

This series is concerned with all aspects of language in education
from the primary school to the tertiary sector. Its authors are
experienced educators who examine both principle and practice of
English subject teaching and language across the curriculum in the
context of current educational and societal developments.

TITLES IN THE SERIES

CHILDREN TALK ABOUT BOOKS:

SEEING THEMSELVES AS READERS

Donald Fry

Open University Press

Milton Keynes · Philadelphia

Open University Press
Celtic Court
22 Ballmoor
Buckingham MK18 1XW
and
1900 Frost Road, Suite 101
Bristol, PA 19007, USA

First Published 1985. Reprinted 1990

British Library Cataloguing in Publication Data

Fry, Donald
    Children talk about books: seeing themselves as readers. —
    (English language and education)
    1. Children — Great Britain — Books and reading
    I. Title   II. Series
    028.5′5   Z1037.A1

    ISBN 0–335–15032–2

Library of Congress Cataloging in Publication Data

Fry, Donald.
    Children talk about books: seeing themselves as readers.
    Includes index.
    1. Children — England — Books and reading — Case studies.
    I. Title.
    Z1037.A1F79   1985   028′.9′042   85–3008

    ISBN 0–335–15032–2

Printed in Great Britain by St Edmundsbury Press Ltd,
Bury St Edmunds, Suffolk

Contents

Acknowledgements

In this book I refer to a number of writers working in different fields – literary, psychological, linguistic, educational – and have been interested in the diversity of these sources. Although each chapter tends to draw upon one writer in particular, I do not feel that any one mode of enquiry will arrive at a full understanding of a child's experience of fiction. That understanding will come from an intermingling of different specialist interests. In my own reading, I have only touched upon some of these interests, but sufficiently to know that those interested in children's response to fiction need to range widely in their reading, and that a fully researched enquiry would properly be multi-disciplinary, and eclectic too, within those disciplines.

Our thinking is also shaped, of course, by those with whom we work and with those who share our interests. In my case, I am particularly grateful to Emrys Evans, who guided this enquiry throughout its early life as a dissertation for the English in Education course at the University of Birmingham, both in the year of my secondment by Coventry LEA (during which these conversations with young readers took place), and also in the writing that followed. I have learned a lot, too, from colleagues in Coventry, in my own department at Whitley Abbey School, in Coventry NATE, and in conversations with Mike Torbe.

I owe most to Helen, Clayton, Hazel, Karnail, Joanne and Sharon. I am especially grateful to Sharon and Joanne, who gave up so much of their free time, but, as I hope extracts from the transcripts will show, all six were exceptionally helpful and thoughtful in their comments to me. I am grateful, too, to their teachers: school life is hectic, but they always found time to arrange meetings, supply me with extra material and information, and encourage me by their interest.

Finally, my thanks to Leonie, and our children Anne and Katherine, to whom this book, for many reasons, is dedicated.

General Editor's Introduction

Donald Fry is Head of the English Department in a comprehensive school in Coventry. This book grows in part out of his experience there and, in particular, out of research undertaken as part of an in-service course. It is a good example of the kind of reflective awareness of the nature of one's teaching that the best kind of classroom research can lead to.

What particularly impressed me when I first saw the draft typescript was the way in which the original perceptions of the children interviewed and discussed were related to theoretical material on reading that has been developed in this country and abroad. Fry has developed an effective capacity to test theoretical ideas against his own considerable experience and in this way to make theory directly usable by the teacher in the classroom. In doing this he has rendered a particular service to his fellow teachers and fulfilled the intentions that lie behind this series as a whole.

But the real 'stars' of the book are, of course, the children themselves who talk about their reading. Transcripts do not always make the easiest of reading but, in this case, the extracts that Fry presents to us have a freshness and interest of their own in the insights that the subjects have into the process of their own reading. There are too few books which take children as seriously as this and recognise them as able to reflect upon the educative process through which they are developing. It is also an index of Donald Fry's skills as a teacher and, above all, as a listener that the children spoke as copiously and feelingly about the reading on which they had been engaged.

The range of reading that the children's conversations reveal is itself interesting and surprising. They show themselves to have clearly developed tastes and to base their reading on values not unlike those of critical adults.

It is difficult to see how the insights developed here through the particular case studies of individual pupils could have been presented by means of more structured or quantitative research. Nonetheless such studies need to be placed alongside such work as that of Frank Whitehead and his colleagues in the survey they published under the title, 'Children's Reading Habits', conducted for the Schools Council. It is in the light of that more global picture that the remarkable nature of Fry's studies is demonstrated.

Uniquely, he brings together his own and the children's insights into the chosen books, his awareness of much work that has been done on the reading process, and a sympathetic understanding of the children who are his subjects. It is to be hoped that other teachers will follow the example of the research presented here.

Perhaps what this book demonstrates above all is the importance for us, as teachers, to learn to listen to children.

Anthony Adams

1 Context

This book reports conversations with six young readers over a period of eight months: 8-year-old Clayton and Helen, 12-year-old Hazel and Karnail, and 15-year-old Joanne and Sharon. This is not a survey of children's reading, taking as its subject a large representative sample; nor is it a study of a smaller, but more manageable group, such as a class in school. It deliberately restricts itself to six young readers in the belief that such case-studies are revealing and helpful because of their particularity, and in the hope that their value will increase as they join, and are joined by, other similar studies of individual readers.

The readers in this study are from three different age-groups. I intended that their ages should be widely spaced, but the fact that I worked with pupils in first-year juniors, first and fifth-year secondary, rather than in other years in school, was simply the result of what it was possible to arrange with their teachers.

To work with children of different ages seemed likely to be more interesting, because of the variety in the children themselves, their schools and teachers, their reading environment, the books they were reading, and in the conversations we would have. But also, of course, when we talk to readers of different ages, we are reminded that each person's reading has a past and future, which are part of the experience of reading: the variety in ages provides the opportunity for some reflections on reading development, and there is an interest in seeing similarities and differences between these readers, between those of the same age, and those who are younger or older.

These are reports on conversations, not interviews. At times, in the transcripts they read like interviews, because of the persistence of the questioning; but these questions were asked in the shared knowledge that what we were trying to discover was what happens when we read, and arose from exchanges about the books the children had just read or were still reading. I had no questionnaire: there were no questions I wanted to put to all the readers, but there were questions I found I wanted to ask about reading particular books.

1

Although it is possible for an interview to be informal, conversation seems to leave more possibilities open for unexpected insights and changes in direction. It also creates a different relationship between the participants: at its best, the speakers help each other by sharing memories and impressions, exchanging anecdotes, comparing responses, and so on. The transcripts will show these conversations to be flawed in ways that will be familiar to all those who have studied tapes of their own talk with children. Even so, the young readers in this study all make valuable statements about reading which I feel would not have been said in any other context but conversation.

Each conversation lasted between 30 and 45 minutes, and I tried to meet each reader several times during the school year: these are important features of the design of the study. I wanted all six to talk about themselves as readers, and to become used to such talk. It needed more than one occasion for this to be possible, and for the potential of such conversation to be fully realised.

The original intention was to arrange to meet while the reading of a particular book was still in progress, as well as when it had been completed, but this often proved difficult: readers sometimes finish books more quickly than they at first thought, or give them up, or have other demands made upon their time. However, the number of conversations did make it possible to discuss the same book more than once, to refer back to previous remarks, and to accommodate uncertainties and changes as a view of a reading experience emerged. It also made possible, of course, discussion of a reader's experience of more than one book, so that we are able to observe a pattern of reading interest over several months, and detect in that pattern significant shifts.

In finding the children with whom to work, I spoke first to three teachers I already knew: they worked in three schools in different sectors of the city. All three teachers were enthusiastic readers themselves and especially interested in children's fiction and what their classes were reading. This study owes a great deal to these teachers – Barbara Brown, Gill Frith and Hilary Minns – first, in the practical help they gave in making the conversations possible; secondly, in their provision of information about the readers, drawn from their day-to-day work in the classroom, and their generous sharing of insights about their pupils; and thirdly, in the interest they themselves generated in their classes for books and the pleasure of reading.

Before we thought about particular children, we chose classes for me to visit, fitting in with the organisation of the school day and the teachers' timetables and patterns of work. The headteachers of the three schools kindly gave me permission to work with the children in their schools.

The approach to the children was different in each of the three schools. I made a first visit to Helen and Clayton's school, Clifford Bridge Junior School, in October, spending the morning in the area where the first-year juniors were working: this gave everyone the chance to see me, and the introduction was made more formally at the end-of-session story-reading by Hilary Minns. Those children who were interested in working with me later signed a notice in the area, and when I next came, a fortnight later, I spoke to all 14, mostly in pairs, although Clayton came on his own. Hilary and I agreed it would be best to invite Helen and Clayton to help: they seemed to have selected themselves.

I also made a full morning visit to Sidney Stringer School, and spent the time with a first-year tutor group who had humanities for the whole morning session. There was plenty of opportunity to talk to the children about reading and stories, as well as to join in the work at their tables. Their teacher, Barbara Brown, who was also their tutor, suggested that when I next came we should simply ask for volunteers – which is what we did. In fact, Barbara had already spoken to Hazel, but the choice of Karnail was unexpected. After the first conversation, both agreed to meet me again.

Sharon and Joanne were both in the fifth year of Tile Hill Wood girls' comprehensive school. Their English teacher, Gill Frith, arranged for me to come to one of her lessons. I explained to the class what it was I was hoping to do and answered questions; we then spent the rest of the lesson in small groups talking about books and reading so that everyone could get some idea of what the conversations with me would involve. As these girls were heavily committed to work in their examination year, we thought it especially important that they should have time to think before offering to help me. We left it that anyone who was interested should let their teacher know, and she would then arrange for them to meet me in school to discuss it further. Joanne and Sharon, who were not part of the same working group in class, both volunteered.

The preliminary visits to each school were important in that they gave the pupils the opportunity to form some impression of me, before deciding whether to take part in the project. They could see, too, that I was a colleague of their teacher and shared her interest in books and reading. But the visits also gave me the chance to work out practicalities of recording and timing in advance; and, more important, to see the children at work in the context of their classrooms, something I did not observe again, as the conversations took place in private in other rooms.

I want to mention briefly some features of book provision in each of the three schools. Books were everywhere at Clifford Bridge, a small, attractive open-plan primary school: they were displayed in a variety of ways, but always invitingly to children. It was easy for children to collect books from their own area and other parts of the school. Picture books and young children's fiction had replaced texts from reading schemes, and alongside these were booklets of the children's own work, which were borrowed and enjoyed just as much as other stories. Karnail and Helen's classroom at Sidney Stringer was very different from this: at that time, the school's first-year were housed in a separate building some way from the main site, in old-fashioned classrooms surrounding a central hall. There were some books in the classroom, but nothing like the attractive class library of fiction that Barbara would have liked. Just across the hall, only seconds away from the classroom, however, was a newly converted library and resources area, with its own helpful staff. The children frequently made use of that, and were obviously at home there. At Tile Hill Wood, the school library was just as encouraging to readers (the librarian also ran a school bookshop). The English Department had set up class libraries in each of its rooms; and the literature examination, assessed by course work (as was the language exam) and taught in mixed-ability groups, made it possible for there to be more choice and variety in reading, and in writing about reading, than in traditional set-books examinations.

I had five conversations with Clayton, Joanne and Sharon, four with Karnail, three with Helen, and just two with Hazel; all the conversations were recorded. My routine, after listening to a tape, was to listen again making detailed notes, including transcriptions of remarks that served as particular reminders of the quality of the conversation. I added to these notes as I listened to the tape again, and to other tapes in the series. Later, I made full transcripts of passages from the tapes. Each chapter in this book draws upon those notes and quotes extracts from the transcripts; but in the course of writing, I have often found myself going back to the tapes themselves in an attempt to recollect more truly the words of these young readers.

Each chapter deals with one of the readers in this study. There are three elements in the description of each reader: first, a characterisation of each as a reader in terms of observable readerly behaviour – what we can see of their transactions with books; second, an account of each reader's experience of one or more books read during the time of the conversations – what it is that engages the reader's interest and gives pleasure; third, a further characterisation of each reader in terms of their particular involvement with fiction – what kind of activity is reading for each of them, and what is its place in their lives.

These young readers are themselves, not representatives of their age-group or of stages of reading development or of approaches to books. Something of what happens in each meeting of reader and book is unrepeatable. The value of a case-study is not that it allows us to establish a type, but that it provides us with a reference point in helping us to characterise other individuals. It clearly would be quite wrong to assume that all children of Helen's age will read *The Shrinking of Treehorn* in the same way (and the example of Rachel demonstrates this), just as it would be wrong to make a similar assumption from Clayton and *Watership Down*, Hazel and *The Little House in the Big Woods*, Karnail and *Well Done Secret Seven*, Joanne and *The Rats*, or Sharon and *Shardik*. But there are likely to be some features in common between these readers' experiences and those of other readers of the same books, and we are more alert to what is individual, if we have reference points such as these case-studies. I think there is also a value in matching our own experience of these books against those of the young readers here: as readers ourselves, we are interested in our own responses; and as people interested in children's reading, we want to know what we still have in common with young readers and in what ways we are different.

Although I have been especially interested in the individual personality of each reader, I have taken the opportunity in each chapter to discuss a topic familiar to those interested in children's reading. The chapter on Helen offers some suggestions why readers choose to return to books many times, re-reading; that on Clayton shows how a child who only reads information books comes to find a value in fiction; Karnail's reading of Enid Blyton is described in the context of an explanation of why Blyton is so attractive to young readers; Hazel's enjoyment of stories is offered as a counterbalance to professorial views of reading as an academic activity; the chapter on Joanne comments on the interests she shares with many other young people, the reading of horror stories and the enjoyment of films; and in Sharon's case, the more general topic is the move from children's fiction into adult books.

In the last chapter, I have drawn out some of the implications of the title-phrase 'seeing themselves as readers', and have suggested ways in which reading fiction is a form of learning. Towards the end of a book such as this, there is a pressure to arrive at conclusions and to make recommendations about practice in schools. I have wanted to comment upon the help adults can give young readers, but generally I have been reluctant to make specific suggestions for teachers. These young readers say things that bear upon our own reading, and upon our responsiveness to our own children as readers and to those we teach. They make us more alert to possibilities and opportunities in talking to children about books, and in working with them: what we actually decide to do is for us to devise, and cannot be had upon prescription.

Note on the transcripts

In making the transcripts, I have used a number of signs:

/	to indicate where a speaker pauses (not necessarily a grammatical break);
. . .	to mark an omission or a cut in the transcript;
(. . .?)	to substitute for words that are indecipherable on tape.

I am well aware that I have not solved the problem of transcription. Even the tapes themselves are distant from the original conversations: the transcripts more so, no matter how they are transposed.

I have selected a number of longer extracts from the transcripts, and these are to be found at the end of the book. These I have punctuated more to make them readable rather than register every pause on the original tapes.

2　Helen

Helen was 8-years-old when I first met her, in the first year of her junior school. She was one of the 14 children in her class who talked to me on my second visit to the school: she quickly showed her interest in books and how much she enjoyed talking about her reading. After the visit, she wrote me a letter giving me more information about herself, and we decided to ask her if she would be willing to help in the project.

After my first conversation with Helen, she was joined by Rachel, as Helen wanted her company. I talked with Helen once, Rachel once when Helen was away from school, and the two together on two other occasions. The conversations usually lasted about half an hour.

This chapter is about Helen's particular interest in two books which she read over and over again, and attempts to explain why she is repeatedly drawn to them. It also mentions Rachel, who shared Helen's enjoyment in one of the books, but found the other 'boring'.

Helen was at ease with books and confident in their presence. I placed a selection of stories in front of her: some she recognised, and said she had already read; others she handled deftly, gathering information as she glanced at the covers and flicked through the pages. Often she assigned a book to a category: animal stories; baby books; ghostly stories; books with too many boys; country stories. As soon as it seemed that a book belonged to a category which held no appeal for her, that book was dismissed.

Her teacher had been reading to the class *The House of Wings*, by Betsy Byars, which Helen did not like. She explained: 'Some books you like and some books you don't like and there's one I don't like.' She knows her own mind: books are accepted or rejected. She has a power over books which she cannot have when dealing with people, and this authority can improve her standing in the world. In a picture she sent me, Mr Fry, in diminutive form, is asking 'Is that the one?', while Helen stands in front of a display of books, pointing.

Of the 14 children I interviewed at her school, Helen was the one child who revealed a marked sense of books belonging to her. Later, she said: 'I buy books, and I just like admiring them.' She is knowledgeable about books, and is not shy of making use of this to attract some admiration towards herself. 'When I read a book what no one's read,' she told me, 'I go and show off and say that bit's dead good!'

When I first met her, Helen's enthusiasm was for stories about witches and wizards, and generally she preferred stories of magic that are about 'things what happen to people' and where people 'change into things'. In *The House of Wings*, things do, of course, happen and people do change, but as far as Helen is concerned nothing happens in the book except 'all walking' and 'running away'. Her friend Rachel said to us, 'I thought the house would really have wings so it could fly away', and this would have been a much more interesting story for both of them.

Bettelheim (1978, pp. 53–54) writes:

> Strictly realistic stories run counter to the child's inner experiences; he will listen to them and maybe get something out of them, but he cannot extract much personal meaning from them that transcends obvious content.

Following Piaget, he suggests that children are convinced by magic, because it conforms to the animistic principles of their thinking.

In the particular case of *The House of Wings*, I am not sure why Helen should express no interest; but it may be that for some children – and I think this is what Bettelheim would argue – the story represents certain fears too visibly. It opens with a small boy, crying and breathless, hiding from his grandfather, who, at this stage in the story, is just a voice shouting 'Boy'. On the second page, he calls to the boy: 'Listen, boy, your mom and dad didn't leave you because they wanted to', to which the boy shouts back, 'Liar! liar!'. (Clayton, however, who is in the same class as Helen, and who is the subject of the next chapter, enjoyed the story, and borrowed it from the teacher to take home.)

I talked to Helen about two stories which were particular favourites, and which she had re-read many times: *The Magic Finger* by Roald Dahl, and *The Shrinking of Treehorn* by Florence Parry Heide. Both stories have emerged from the fairy world, but they are not part of the world of naturalist fiction. The transformations that occur in the stories are magical in that they defy what we know to be possible, but they occur in settings that we recognise as close to our own.

Helen borrowed *The Shrinking of Treehorn* from school, and kept it for about a month. During that time she read the story 'nine times in bed and one time in school'. She has read *The Magic Finger*, which is her own book, 18 times – she keeps a record.

What explains this desire to read a book again and again? When you read a story many times, it becomes as familiar as the bed in which you sleep and the house in which you live: what was just a book becomes a story that particularly belongs to you. The book itself becomes an object that is especially familiar to you and, years later, taken from the shelf, it can speak to you of your own past as well as tell its own story.

The re-reading of a book often establishes for the reader little routines. Clayton avoids looking at the last small picture in *The Snowman*, which shows the boy looking at the melted man: 'Usually when I do it I don't look at the end page . . . I always turn it over to the white page.' Helen, as part of the routine of re-reading *Treehorn*, closes the book: 'Every time I finish the book I turn to the back cover and see his face green.' This little custom is one of the ways in which she makes the book her own. A casual reader of the book may not notice this small feature on the back cover, but Helen knows it is there as she re-reads the story, and, sure enough, as she turns the page to close the book there is Treehorn's green face. She knows, and yet the knowledge does not become stale: it is as though Treehorn only turns green when Helen turns the page.

When you have read a story many times, it is almost as though you know it as well as the person who wrote it; when you tell it to someone else, it could almost be your own story. You have become the authority on the story. You can be sure, too, that your knowledge will not become obsolete: the story does not change. There is even the possibility of so knowing a story that the memory of it is complete without the reminder of the text: each re-reading is a further graft of the story from the book to the reader, until at the nth re-reading it finally takes.

But the story resists and finally rejects remembrance. Helen says of *Treehorn*: 'Each night I read it / I read the whole book / and then 'cos I forgot about it 'cos I went to sleep . . . I forgot about it and kept reading it.' Every time she returns to the book, familiar though it is, there is some new detail which either she overlooked before or now sees in a different way. Part of our interest in re-reading is in observing the play between what happens and our memory of what happens – a pleasing match or a disconcerting mismatch. We often think of predictability as a deficiency in a story, but it can be part of a reader's satisfaction.

Even when we do not re-read a story, our reading depends upon our knowledge that the story is re-readable. We know that we can find our place again, turn back to check on something, offer the story to someone else to read. We know that we can return to a story in print, if not now, then later, when we have more time, years later perhaps. This part of our past is recoverable.

Above all, we know that we can always turn back to the beginning, and, as readers, renew our experience. Clayton cannot avoid the sad ending of *The Snowman*, but he can, and does, 'go back': on the front cover, the snowman smiles back at him again. We read not only with a sense of an ending, but with the option of beginning again.

Possessing, remembering, reproducing, renewing – I think these are some of the activities that could underlie a child's constant re-reading of a story. But this does not explain why a particular book holds such an attraction for a particular child. What I want to discover is not why Helen re-reads books, but why she re-reads these two books, *Treehorn* and *The Magic Finger*.

Helen says, 'I forgot about it and kept reading it.' All of us find ourselves forgetting what we have read. We cannot hold the whole of a text in our heads: its length makes it impossible for it to be available to us in that way. Further, if our grasp of a story were that complete – so that all events and moments in the story were equally memorable – we would have difficulty making sense of it: that some parts are more memorable than others is our first move in reflecting upon what we read. Helen does not forget the book: it is just that she remembers some parts more clearly and accurately than others. We would expect this of any reader and any book. We know that some moments, because of the way they are placed in the telling of a story, will be memorable to the majority of readers. But what a reader remembers is governed as much by her own nature as the nature of the story. When we ask why Helen remembers some parts of the story more readily than others, and wants to talk about these, we come at a purpose for re-reading beyond what has so far been suggested.

I want to agree with Bettelheim again:

> I have known parents whose child reacted to a fairy story by saying 'I like it', and so they moved on to telling another one, thinking that an additional tale would increase the child's enjoyment. But the child's remark, as likely as not, expresses an as yet vague feeling that this story has got something important to tell him – something that will get lost if the child is not given repetition of the story and time to grasp it . . . The child should be given the opportunity to slowly make a fairy tale his own by bringing his own associations to and into it.
>
> (Bettelheim, 1978, p. 59)

When Helen returns again and again to *Treehorn* and *The Magic Finger*, she re-reads the story, which does not change, in order to think about herself, who does change and is changing. Indirectly, the story speaks to her about herself. Re-reading is a process of familiarisation whereby Helen comes into possession of a story and, to some extent, her own self.

When Treehorn turns green, he says to himself: 'I don't think I'll tell anyone. If I don't say anything they won't notice.' He has learned from his experience of shrinking: adults do not notice his predicament, and when their attention is drawn to him they can only react by ignoring, reproving, patronising or blaming him. Helen began by telling me about this:

Helen   He / gets smaller and then when it / at the end of it he gets green. 'I won't tell anybody, I'll keep it to myself.'

DF   Why doesn't he tell anybody? Because it looks pretty awful, if you've got green / and his hands are green too, now I look closely.

Helen   Because um / what happened / to / him when he shrinked / everybody knew about it and kept fussing / so probably he doesn't want / anybody to / probably fuss about it when he turns green.

DF   When you say everybody / who is everybody in the story?

Helen   His mum and dad and the doctor and everything.

Part of the fun of the story is that Treehorn remains calm while the adults fuss. He eventually finds his own solution, when he finds the game: Helen calls this 'the game of life'.

Helen   When he went back some spaces it says Grow up and he grew up so the / er / game came true.
         . . . The game cured him.

Treehorn is unperturbed and self-sufficient.

Helen   He weren't really bothered. But he kept / his mum didn't take any notice of him. She was in the kitchen and when he came down the first morning when he was shrinking / he tripped over his trousers and his mummy said 'Please watch what you're doing you're going to ruin my cake' / because she's got a cake in the oven and she's not / um / wondering about what he's / saying to her 'cos he's saying 'My trousers are getting too long my sleeves are getting too long' and she's saying / 'Be quiet this cake won't turn out right'. That's all she's saying to him.

DF   So she's more worried about the cake than

Helen   Yes more worried about the cake than him.

DF   So she's not / I mean / she's not really fussing then is she? She's not worried either.

Helen   No. And then that night she's really fussing about it.

DF   Oh I see.

Helen   She says Call a doctor or something / to the father. 'He is really shrinking now. What shall we do?'

Helen tells this with much enjoyment, putting on a voice for the mother's words. It is the first of five times in the half-hour that Helen tells or refers to this part of the story, and she chooses the drawing that accompanies it as her favourite page. For example, towards the end of the interview, when I am thinking of ending, she returns to it once more:

DF   You think you might read it again one day.

Helen   Yes.
         [A pause of 7 seconds]

But when the bit she comes in she didn't / um Treehorn comes into the kitchen she doesn't really / um / doesn't really bother about him. She's just bothering about the cake looking at it.

DF   Yes. You like that bit don't you?

Helen   Mmm.

Earlier, Helen said, 'His mum's always worrying over him. It's ever so funny.' Helen's word 'worrying' seems closer here to her word 'fussing': Treehorn's mother worries not so much about him as his appearance, his table manners, his eating, his hair, the volume of the TV he is watching. As Helen says, she is more concerned about the cake and the state of the house than she is about her own son. This is funny, but it is itself worrying, too. Shouldn't a mother be worried when something is wrong with her child? Shouldn't she make a fuss of him or her? Helen finds an analogy in her own recent experience: 'Like your dog is poorly or something and you don't know what is going to happen to it.'

I went on to ask her what she thought of the way grown-ups behave in the book. It is the mother she first thinks of. 'Well the mum didn't behave very good.' She says her own mother 'would have tried to get a doctor quickly or something like that'. Once, she let the washing machine overflow when she was on the phone: she wouldn't have bothered about the cake!

Helen does tell me other parts of the story. In her first run at telling the story, she does not mention the mother at all until the end of the story: 'His mum comes in and says Brush your hair and he looks in the mirror and he's turned green.' But I think it is the relationship between Treehorn and his mother that particularly puzzles and bothers her, and helps to explain why she returns to the story many times.

In the story, she recognises, although they are safely and funnily exaggerated, facts of her own life and wishful thinking. She wants to avoid being fussed over and nagged at, and to feel herself in control of situations; but at the same time she wants the adults in her life to care for her and take command, especially when she is in distress. *The Shrinking of Treehorn* plays out that dilemma as many times as she cares to view it.

In a last section of transcript from the end of this conversation, Helen tells the story of a time when she was ill. I cannot help associating this with the story of Treehorn, although I recognise that these associations are based only on supposition.

DF   . . . You like that bit don't you?

Helen   Mmm.

    [A pause of 7 seconds]

DF   Have you ever had anything wrong with you / that worried you?

Helen   Um I had German measles the day after we broke up / from the summer holidays . . .

. . . I kept getting spots on me and my mum went to work the next day and / um / my dad was at home / she thought she'd look in at me but she didn't / and then / um / I woke up and my sister and I said / I didn't notice me myself / my sister noticed because she was on the loo and I put my hand round the corner to frighten her and she said Eee you've got spots on your arm look and I had spots everywhere / and it really frightened me and I had to get / my dad was going golfing that day so I had to go to my nan's . . .

. . . He was worried about he could / he should have looked after me or nan or gone golfing / but he went golfing and my nan looked after me / and when I came home / my mum already knew and I hid my face on the pillow so she wouldn't see. When she came in / I know you've got / she said 'I know you've got German measles' and I was ever so frightened about it. . . .

. . . I thought I was going to die or something / because / er / you're itching everywhere. . . .

DF   How long were you frightened for?
Helen   A day and night. I wouldn't go to sleep. I kept fretting. I kept saying 'Mum will I die?'
DF   And what did your mum say?
Helen   No. She kept putting me back to bed, up and down the stairs, but I kept coming down and she kept coming up.
DF   Did she think you were being silly or was she.
Helen   She didn't think I was being silly, 'cos I was really frightened, and she said, 'Well you won't die will you dear. Go back to bed.'
DF   So she tried to comfort you did she?
Helen   Yes. Then she read me a story, and I went to sleep.
DF   Mmm. What did she read you?
Helen   My favourite book. Magic Finger.

Helen's friend Rachel had also borrowed *The Shrinking of Treehorn*, but her response is very different from Helen's. At first she was interested in the book, but after a few pages it became 'a bit boring'. Why was that?

Rachel I was rather disappointed when I looked at this page / when he found the / er / game.
DF   What's happening there?
Rachel I think he's playing a game. It must be a game / because it says / for kids to grow on / I was a bit disappointed when I saw that.
DF   Can you say why? What's wrong with that?
Rachel I wanted him to grow smaller and smaller. I didn't want him to grow bigger and bigger.

Although Rachel is attracted by the idea of 'shrinking', it is not developed in the way that she would find most satisfying. This is partly because she wants to play with the idea and take it, with ingenuity, to its furthest.

> Rachel   I wanted him to grow smaller and smaller and smaller until he was as small as a pinhead.
>
> DF   Why did you want that to happen? Wouldn't that be / he'd be in danger if he got that small, wouldn't he?
>
> Rachel   Mmm.
>
> DF   If he were that small, he might get lost.
>
> Rachel   For I would get lost. I wouldn't know where I was even when I was in my house. Covers would be too big for me when I got into bed. I'd have to jump and jump and jump until I have to get into bed.
>
> DF   And you'd get lost inside the bed.
>
> Rachel   Mmm / and the hot water bottle would be too hot for me.

Despite my word 'danger', Rachel elaborates playfully upon the implications of shrinking. But the story restricts the play of her imagination, because Treehorn only goes so far, then grows again, and turns green!

Her conversion of my 'he' to her 'I' ('For I would get lost') shows who she really has in mind:

> DF   Do you ever think of yourself getting smaller?
>
> Rachel   No. I want to be smaller but I'm not!
>
> DF   Why would you want to be smaller?
>
> Rachel   So that I can go into the playgroup.
>
> DF   Why? Because it's nice in there?
>
> Rachel   Mmm. We play things / play with things / and read books / and you don't have to do any work.

(The same school building houses the juniors, the infants and the playgroup. Rachel liked to go to the infants area to read, as she found it quieter there.)

> DF   . . . Do you ever have dreams about being small?
>
> Rachel   I dream of shrinking. My mum said / my mum said I have to go / I have to go to the playgroup, so she took me to the playgroup and the next day I grew big again and I had to go back into the school.
>   . . .
> DF   Was it a funny dream, a sad dream?
>
> Rachel   A sad dream / going back into normal size.

The story of Treehorn fails to satisfy her, because it cannot improve upon her dream: she wanted to use the story to contemplate the possibility of growing down rather than growing up. She wanted Treehorn successfully to defy the norms of the adult world of home and school. I think, at this time, she had particular reasons for this, but it is not an uncommon thought in any of us at any time.

Rachel knows that only a story can make possible the transformation she dreams of:

DF   Is it possible for someone to shrink?
Rachel No. [She laughs]
DF   So how is it that he shrinks?
Rachel It's just a made-up story.

But *The Shrinking of Treehorn* is the wrong story, as it does not meet either her imaginative or her emotional expectations. Hence, it is 'a bit boring'.

The girl in *The Magic Finger* exclaims early in the story (p. 8), 'I can't stand hunting. I just can't stand it. It doesn't seem right to me that men and boys should kill animals just for the fun they get out of it.' But what can she do? When she talks to the boys who are shooting, they laugh at her, and Mr Gregg walks past her 'as if I weren't there'. Helen knows how she feels:

Helen I get cross when / it's summer and the birds come and lay their eggs because all the people up our road want the eggs / and the mother's there and they frighten them away and get the eggs. I get really cross.
DF   What / boys and girls go after
Helen We were going to the dentist yesterday / and my mum / saw this lady trip up / she was old and she goes / and we was too late / and my mum and this other lady (. . . ?) and took her to the shop.
DF   And they helped her.
Helen Yes.
        [A pause of 5 seconds]
        I'm not much of a help.

She shares the girl's anger, but she also recognises that feeling of helplessness in which a child seems able only to stand and watch. What could she do to stop the stealing of eggs? Whereas Rachel suggests that she would frighten people by putting on her monster mask, Helen says, 'I'd get my dad, 'cos he gets cross when there are some people doing things like taking eggs away.'

In the story, the girl is able to take action herself: she has a magic finger. When she is angry 'a sort of flash comes out of me, a quick flash, like something electric. It jumps out and touches the person who has made me cross' (p. 15). Ducks and Greggs change places, and it is the Greggs who are in danger of being shot. Helen enjoys this reversal of roles, particularly the picture where the young ducks are playing with the toy train in the Greggs' house.

Funny though it is, the story has its menacing aspects. Both Helen and Rachel are attracted by the idea of possessing a magic finger; but the story is clear about its danger. The girl says, 'I saw red. And before I was able to stop myself, I did something I never meant to do' (p. 10).

> *DF*   If you had a magic finger / I don't know how much she can
>   control it you see. She gets angry as you said, and gets cross and
>   it all goes red.
>
> *Helen*   I don't think she can control it! Every time she gets angry / every
>   time I get angry with my sister I think like / going to get a knife
>   and *kill* her.
>
> *Rachel* I get sh. . . sometimes I'm going to get the sharpest knife out of
>   the cupboard / and then I go upstairs, my sister's there / my
>   sister's up there and I pretend I'm going to kill her.

In the story, the girl cries, 'Oh that Magic Finger! What has it done to
my friends?' Helen has a similar thought when she considers anger she
cannot control:

> *Helen*   I wouldn't like that. 'Cos I might get / I might get / um / cross with
>   my friend and just go / oh no / you know / something like that
>   would happen / *awful* / something awful would happen.

I think Helen's first delight in *The Magic Finger* is the fun of its
turnaround, serve-them-right story. But I suspect that, in Bettelheim's
phrase, she 'brings her own associations to it': her feelings of powerless-
ness to intervene in the world and her feelings of terrible anger.

The story also raises an issue important to Helen: how we treat
animals. Towards the end of this interview, she tells Rachel and me of
her friend's brother, who takes eggs from a nest only when he is sure
they have been abandoned, and then hatches and rears the young birds.
'I think that's good,' Helen said seriously. Her re-reading of the story
now marks her developing interest in the world around her and in the
forming of judgements of what is right and wrong.

I need to end this chapter with some back-tracking. I have tried to
suggest that these books are important to Helen because they enable her
to ponder upon aspects of her own experience: in re-reading, she is
reviewing and reconsidering things that intrigue her because they are
part of her sense of herself as a growing person. I am not sure whether I
have identified these aspects accurately: probably I have read too much
into what Helen has said. But I do believe that stories are useful, indeed
necessary, to Helen in this way, just as they are to all of us at some times.

The books, too, are funny, and that should not be lost sight of. Like
many in her class, Helen likes books that make her laugh – laugh out
loud. Much of talking about books is like sharing a lovely joke; and each
re-reading is a fresh occasion for laughter.

3 Clayton

I met Clayton on my first visit to Clifford Bridge Junior School. It just happened that we sat together in the same corner of the 'area', and it was Clayton who explained to me the organisation of the school day and the contents of his 'tray'. We spent most of the morning together: he talked to me about his project on tractors, showed me the books in his tray, and we also looked at some of the many books displayed around the school, many of them made by the children.

Clayton signed the notice in the classroom to say he was interested in working with me, and on my second visit came to talk to me on his own, rather than with a friend like the others. He seemed to have selected himself, and the choice of Clayton was further confirmed by the fact that his teacher knew him particularly well, having taught him in the Infants. When we asked him if he would be willing to help, he agreed.

I had five conversations with Clayton, each about half an hour, the first in December and the last in June. During that time, Clayton (who had just had his eighth birthday when I first met him) read *Watership Down*: this chapter is mainly about that reading. I say 'read', though in fact it is difficult to be sure just how much of the book Clayton read silently to himself; but certainly he came to know it very well, and became the class authority on the story.

This chapter is about how a beginning reader (who in the previous year had been working with a member of the city's remedial reading team) became absorbed in a demanding text with the support of home and school; and, more than other chapters in this study, describes the classroom practices that encouraged this reading. It is also about a child who found how important a story could be for him, and so began to see the place of literature in his life.

A 'story' by Clayton usually began 'One day I was going to the farm'. Here is one he wrote at the beginning of his second year in junior school, some months after my last interview with him:

> One day I was going to the farm and he was combining and I had to go
> and get the cows off, and I went to get a tractor and trailer to go back.

'He' is his father, who, when Clayton was seven, had spent a year at
agricultural college; it seemed to me that Clayton was busy turning his
experience of school into his own small version of his father's studies.
Here are some extracts from his teachers' records:

> *April–July 1977* (in the Infants)
> . . . Always writing about farming. . . . can write interesting stories. Prefers
> to write about farming.

> *Autumn Term 1978* (in the Juniors)
> Clayton has been reading farming books. He tells me he reads *Farmer's
> Weekly* at home. . . . Clayton's writing is mainly factual – about farming.
> He's written two letters to tractor companies . . .

A year later, he is still at it: 'I have started a new topic on farming' he
mentions in a letter he sent.

Clayton's teacher does not stand in the way of this: she sees here
many opportunities for the advancement of his writing and reading, and
appreciates the personal importance of the topic for Clayton. His work
may seem repetitive, but the teacher guides the writing into a variety of
forms, encouraging Clayton to think of the various people to whom and
for whom he is writing. (One of his 'projects', for example, was an
information booklet for his father about 'bugs', which he then took
home.) Clayton takes up these suggestions because he knows there is a
real interest in what he is doing, from his teacher and from his
classmates, all of whom share their work and pool their 'books' as part of
the resources of their classroom.

His teacher was worried, though, that Clayton had no time for stories,
and seemed not to value them. The first 'story-book' that Clayton told
me about was the programme for the Royal Smithfield Show in London,
which he had visited with his father; his conversation about that trip was
almost entirely in the form of giving me information – names of
machinery, information about animals, a list of the firms on display – not
the anecdotal narrative I had expected when I asked him to tell me the
story of his day out.

Like many children, Clayton was securing his own pieces of territory
within the province of knowledge, and, within his own small community
at least, he had established his rights. As he explained his project,
showed me the books in his tray, told me about the Show, it was as
though he were guiding me around what he knew. I was duly impressed
by his knowledge, both first hand from his experience of working on the
farm with his father, and what he had gathered from reading. For the
time being, establishing this expertise was his priority.

Clayton did read stories – the classroom was full of them, invitingly displayed; and he enjoyed the stories the teacher regularly read to the class. But stories were pastimes, not part of the serious business of learning. If I had been Clayton's teacher, I might well have intervened, and foisted more fiction upon him; but in fact his teacher waited, trusting that, because story-books were all around him and story-telling an everyday occurrence in the class, Clayton would come to value a story in his own time for his own reasons. She was right.

In the autumn term when I visited the school, one of the most popular books in the school was Raymond Briggs's *The Snowman*. As I mentioned in the previous chapter, this became one of Clayton's favourite books.

Clayton	. . . I like that bit where he runs and flies / takes off. And this is my favourite / the sad part / when he melts at the end.
DF	Yes. Yes it is a bit sad isn't it.
Clayton	Yes. Usually when I / when I do it I don't look at the end page.
DF	Why?
Clayton	It's so sad.
DF	What / when you read this book you don't look at the last page?
Clayton	No. I always turn it over to the white / to the white pages and then go back.
DF	Even though you know what's on the page.
Clayton	Yes.
DF	I took it down as a present to a little boy of a friend of mine in Wales and he's only three and a half and he got to the last page / I thought he was going to cry / because he was a bit sad about it.
Clayton	Did he?
DF	No / he sort of said Ooooh / he sort of groaned like that you know. He sounded really upset.

Clayton's question 'Did he?' is not casual: he is interested in the little boy's response, just as he is interested in the way the picture story makes him feel. The story made an impression upon him – he had a copy at home as well – and, in response to a suggestion from his teacher, he wrote his own story to send to Raymond Briggs.

One day I went out and I saw it was snowing and I made a snowman and I went to my breakfast and then I went to see my snowman and I went to bed. And I got up and went to see if my snowman was there and I went to call for my friend and we went back to the snowman and my snowman had moved and we were astonished and we went to my friends house and he made a snowman and we went back to my house to see if my snowman was there but it wasnt there so I went to my friends house but his wasnt there so they had melted.

That Clayton wanted to write this story, rather than continue with his pieces about farming, and that he spent so much time on it to write so much, testifies to the effect *The Snowman* had upon him. Yet, in response to a story in which a snowman magically moves, flies, he tells a story in which a snowman he actually made literally moves – for, as Clayton explained, what really happened was that the snowman slid down a slope as it began to melt. And in response, too, to a story which had certainly touched him, he tells a story in a matter-of-fact tone, apparently accepting, unmoved, common everyday facts of real life. It is 'a true story', says Clayton: he answers fiction with fact.

I am suggesting that, although Clayton's story seems to be taking his writing in a new direction, it still occupies the old ground: he is still down on the farm, as it were. But this is a secondary response to his reading of *The Snowman*: his first feelings are acted out in his turning of the final pages. Perhaps his own story is his way of countering his imaginative involvement in the original, and of reconciling his feeling of sadness with his knowledge of how the world really is. What also might be happening is that in recalling the making of his own snowman in response to the snowman he reads about, he is contemplating the possibility of magic: beneath the matter-of-fact snow of his story, there might be a layer of wishful thinking.

It may also be simply that Clayton did not try to write something he would find too difficult: to put into the words of his own story the feelings experienced through the pictures of the original. He had already tried this by telling the story on to a tape-recorder as he turned the pages (an activity which many in the class enjoyed doing, and which is explored further in Appendix A). He began like this:

> One morning I was asleep, the next minute I was awake. I looked out the window and it was snowing. I said Hooray! I dressed as fast as I can. I went downstairs, asked my mother if I could go out. She said Put your hat on, don't forget to put your hat on. I ran outside, my hat fell off, I didn't care . . .

This is not re-telling the story, but actually bringing it to life in words, interpreting action and character through the pictures. Of course, Clayton can do this so effectively here rather than in writing, as he can work at a pace which allows him to improvise with language, and effect an immediate match between what he perceives and what he says. In this situation, he emerges as a skilled story-teller.

> . . . Couldn't get to sleep, put my dressing gown on, sneaked downstairs, looked out the door window, opened the door. The snowman lifted his hat off his head, and started walking towards me. He shook my hand. He said to me 'I am a snowman'. 'Come on in. Do you like fires?' He showed him the fire. He showed him the television. He showed him the light.

'Sneaked' is evidence of Clayton 'reading' the picture; and 'Do you like fires?' shows him humorously working upon the immediate situation in the story and what he knows happens in the end. This part of the story, in which the boy shows the 'man' around his world, pointing out machines and appliances, particularly appealed to Clayton. (Whenever I read the story now, I think of Clayton showing me the books in his tray, and explaining to me about farm machinery.) At this point, 'I' changes to 'he', although later he moves back to the first person:

> . . . I waved to the snowman and put my hand down. I was tossing and turning, awake asleep, awake asleep, kept on tossing and turning. It was morning. I put my dressing gown on, ran downstairs. Without having any breakfast I ran straight past my mum and dad. He had melted.

This is told in a peremptory manner (even though in print the words can be heard more elegiacally); by this time the story-teller is tiring, and wants to move through the pictures more speedily. But from the moment when the snowman soars into the sky holding the boy by the hand, the story has become more difficult to tell: the pictures resist the substitution of words, and the telling becomes more a series of captions than a story in its own right. Just as Clayton senses that he cannot do in writing what he does on tape, so here he does not try to do on tape what Raymond Briggs does in pictures.

It has been possible, then, to see Clayton's response to *The Snowman* moving through a variety of activities: from his handling of the book ('I don't look at the last page . . .'), to his conversations with others, including me, about the book ('the sad part when he melts at the end'), to his own re-creation of the story through telling on tape ('He had melted'), to the writing of his own story ('so they had melted'), almost a rival version. Each of these marks a different stage in the reader asserting himself over the story, and distancing himself from his own first sense of loss as the book ended. 'Response' does not seem to be the outcome of any one of these activities, but a movement within and through them. Nor, surely, does it come to a rest with the story Clayton wrote, but remains toing and froing between his own last sentence and the last page of the book: between sense and sentiment, acceptance and sadness, fact and fantasy.

'Clayton's been very impressed with *The Snowman*', his teacher writes in her record, the first story to be so named since the records began three years ago. About the same time, he took home *The House of Wings*, which the teacher had been reading as a serial to the class. During the Christmas holidays, while he was visiting his grandmother, he came across another picture book that impressed him – the book of the film of the book, *Watership Down*.

His grandmother's book was a Penguin large-format collection of stills from the animated version of *Watership Down* (although Clayton had not yet seen the film). Although the stills are in sequence, they are not intended to tell the whole story, and there are no captions or intervening text: the book is a keepsake of the film. But Clayton 'read' it, and constructed from the pictures his own idea of the story.

He then ordered the original *Watership Down* through the school book club, and there began a routine of regular readings at home. 'I asked my dad to read it,' and Clayton 'watches' the book as his father reads. 'He reads one chapter and then I go over it before we go to bed every night.' We never established exactly what 'going over it' entailed: Clayton might sometimes have read bits back to his father, but probably he mostly read to himself, asking for help on words, when he was 'stuck' (Clayton's word). Whatever really happened, what matters is what Clayton believed he had done: he wrote to me after our last interview, 'I have finished *Watership Down* I read it on my own I felt proud of myself'. This was six months after he first mentioned the story to me.

It would have been sensible to have spoken to Clayton's father – one of those missed opportunities. Margaret Clark, in her study of young fluent readers (1976, p. 97), also regrets not having arranged interviews with all the fathers of the children she studied, and observes:

> . . . in most of the homes both parents played a crucial role in their children's intellectual development and . . . a number of the boys particularly were already modelling their speech and their interests on those of their father. Some of the fathers were attempting to learn new skills stimulated by the enthusiasms of their children.

In Clayton's home there are books about trains, farming, horses and wildflowers. His father becomes interested himself in *Watership Down* and asks if he can borrow it, and, says Clayton, moans because there is not enough quiet. Thus Clayton sees his interest in the book confirmed by his father, and maintained by the regular readings, which, having read ahead, his father does well: Clayton particularly liked the different 'noises' he made for the rabbits.

As his father reads, Clayton matches what he hears with his memory of his grandmother's book: 'I think of the pictures in my head'. Later I gave him a copy of the picture book, which he came to know very well; and, just as earlier he had shown me his books on tractors, now he was able to take others through the pictures in *Watership Down*, telling the story, and finding where he had reached in the 'big book' his father was reading.

The film now arrived in town: Clayton went to see it, of course, and made a large poster for the classroom, advertising it to the other children. The story became very popular, and the teacher set up some drama work in which the children acted it out: part of her thinking here was to capitalise upon Clayton's interest, and encourage him in the new kind of expertise he was developing – he is recognised as the authority on the book.

> DF   How do you decide what to do? [in the play]
> Clayton   Well Miss doesn't know more than me / she says she might go and see the film / and every bit where they've finished a bit that we've done last time she asks / she asks me what happens next. And I say that they go and meet some of the things while the others go and silflay / that's one of the words that Richard Adams made up.

Clayton now has the play, as well as the film and the picture book, to hold against his father's reading aloud, and all of these support him in his own attempts at the 'big book'. (Apart from the story it tells, the book interested Clayton as an object quite unlike any other book he had handled: he liked to see how many chapters there were and how many pages each was, and their titles; he was able to say from memory exactly how long the book is; he had noticed 'those little things before each chapter that you can read'; and, of course, liked the special layout on the page about the noticeboard.)

What must also have been happening is that Clayton was matching original with picture book, film and play, and beginning to develop an awareness of how a story changes through different ways of telling. One could not expect him to be explicit about this, other than to point out discrepancies in what happens in different versions – which he did. The various re-tellings of the story, including his own in conversations with other children and adults, not only assist him in his own silent reading of the text, helping him to picture what he reads and to know what's coming next, but enable him to distinguish what the particular experience of reading is, as compared with other forms of telling. He is learning about reading, as a skill, and as an experience.

Here is an extract from our first conversation about the book (February):

> DF   Can you tell me what's happened so far in the book?
> Clayton   Well / Hazel and Fiver have decided to leave the warren where all the rabbits are and / it started where they were going out for a walk over this bridge and / um / there was this noticeboard and they were going to build on the land. So Hazel and Fiver decided to leave the warren and some more rabbits came along . . .

In passing, it is worth commenting on the effectiveness of this synopsis, and to show that Clayton can both report on a story in this way and re-create it, as in his telling of *The Snowman*.

> DF   Which of the rabbits do you think at the moment you like the best?

> *Clayton*   Um / Hazel.
> *DF*   Yes / why is that?
>   *[10 seconds]*
>   What can you say about Hazel?
>   *[22 seconds]*
>   Is he the kind of / is he the kind of leader or is he one of the / or
>   is he more like Fiver / I can't . . .
>   *[20 seconds]*
> *Clayton*   Er.

This is not quite so laboured as it seems: Clayton has a knack of toying with his interviewer, and he delivers his 'er' (a favourite ploy) not so much as one struggling for an idea, as one resigning himself to answer. Yet, as studies such as Applebee's (1978) have led us to expect, young children do have difficulty in discussing a story once the conversation moves beyond telling what happens. Frank Whitehead (1977) stated, 'The young reader seldom finds it possible to be articulate in any specific way about what he has liked or valued in his reading' – a remark often quoted by those trying to show the opposite!

> *Clayton*   Er.
>   Well / he's the one who always goes / he's the one who tells
>   them all what to do but Fiver asks him if he can / they can leave
>   the warren who (. . .?) and / so they / um / Fiver went collecting /
>   Bigwig went collecting more / um / rabbits / and came back
>   with two.
> *DF*   Is Hazel bossy? You say he tells the others what to do.
> *Clayton*   Well he always goes at the front.
> *DF*   So he's braver than Fiver say?
> *Clayton*   Yes. 'Cos he always goes at the front and Bigwig second Fiver
>   third / um / Hazel fifth / Blackberry last.

He is in some confusion here (which perhaps leads to the slip about 'Hazel fifth'): the actions of all three rabbits – Hazel, Fiver and Bigwig – are characteristic of leadership. His reference to Fiver seems to be correcting my assumption that to be 'more like Fiver' is to be less like a leader.

We came back to this question of leadership a few weeks later (in March): in the meantime, Clayton has read several more chapters at home.

> *DF*   . . . If you think of all the gang of rabbits.
> *Clayton*   Mmmm.
> *DF*   Hazel Pipkin Fiver Bigwig Dandelion Speedwell / and all the
>   others / one of them has to be the leader.
> *Clayton*   Bigwig.
> *DF*   Yes / now is Bigwig the leader do you think?
> *Clayton*   Yes.

DF   Why is that then?
Clayton   Well he orders them all about.
DF   Mmm. Doesn't Hazel order them around though?
Clayton   Not much / no / really Bigwig / much.
DF   Tell me something about Bigwig.
Clayton   Well he / at the end / um / somewhere.
            [Clayton looks through the picture book]
            That's Bigwig I think.
DF   Yes I think it is.
Clayton   Yes that's Bigwig. He comes out of that hole and attacks the
            other one. I'll show you where he kills one. That's where Bigwig
            kills one. Comes out of that hole and bites his neck.
DF   Why is that Bigwig becomes leader. I mean / why doesn't one or
            the others / why not Blackberry or Pipkin or one of those?
Clayton   Pipkin gets took. Took by a bird.
DF   Does he.
Clayton   He's flown off with. He was / here he is took. That's where
            Hazel got shot and he gets all the stuff off him and comes alive
            again. That's where he gets shot.

Here, Clayton is renewing acquaintance with the picture book, which I
gave to him at the beginning of this interview, and which he is now
introducing to me. The illustrations of the fight between Bigwig and
Woundwort are particularly striking, and having them there before him
perhaps influences Clayton in his comments. We go on to imagine an
election in which the rabbits choose their leader: who would Clayton
vote for? His first answer is Fiver – thinking again of the beginning of
the story (and perhaps feeling some affinity with Fiver, the 'child' rabbit
with visionary knowledge) – and then mentions Bigwig.

DF   . . . How would you persuade me to vote for Bigwig?
            Why should he be leader?
Clayton   Oh / he really does boss them about.
DF   Mmm mmm.
            [19 seconds]
            Why does he boss them about? Is he just bossy or is he.
Clayton   No / 'cos he was the leader from the first. Well Hazel / Fiver
            started it off and then Hazel and then / um / came up to Bigwig
            'cos Hazel made / Fiver made Hazel leave the warren.
DF   Yes / so it's Fiver who saw the danger at first. Now where does
            Hazel come into it then?
Clayton   He comes into it when / er / Bigwig / they find Bigwig / he
            comes into it when Bigwig / um / wasn't there. They find Bigwig.
DF   Do you think Hazel wanted to be leader?
Clayton   No not really.
DF   What does Hazel think of Bigwig? Are they friends?
Clayton   Yes. The bird / er / Hazel / the bird was more friends to Hazel
            than Bigwig though / 'cos the bird / um / pulled the bullet out of
            Hazel. He stayed alive to the end.

If the school were doing a play of *Watership Down*, who would Clayton like to play? He nominates Hazel, and goes on to tell the story of the plan whereby the rabbits set the dog loose so that it attacks Woundwort's men: he explains exactly how the plan works, in detail, speaking quite quickly. The ingenuity of Hazel now rivals the physical strength of Bigwig.

DF	Is it Hazel who for the most part thinks up the plans?
Clayton	Yeah.
	. . .
DF	If Bigwig is the leader then he ought to be thinking up some of the plans hadn't he?
Clayton	Hazel thought up most of them though. Bigwig only thought up two.

When the class actually do act out the story (shortly after this), Clayton plays the part of Bigwig. Later he talks about this with his teacher:

T	If you had to choose to be one of those rabbits / just one / which would you be?
Clayton	Bigwig.
T	Like you were in the play. Did you enjoy acting him out?
Clayton	*[nods]*
	. . .
T	Would you have enjoyed being Hazel so much?
Clayton	No.
T	I wonder why.
Clayton	Hazel's a bossy boots.
T	Hazel?
Clayton	Mmm.
T	Can you say a bit more about that?
Clayton	He bosses people around. He thinks up most of the plans but still some of them aren't good.

Playing Bigwig gives Clayton the chance to be at the centre of one of his favourite scenes, where the rabbit is caught in the snare; but it is also an opportunity to play out again the problem of leadership in the book. In the end Clayton decided to write to the author about what was puzzling him.

Dear Richard,
     I like your book of *Watership Down*.
Why do you call Hazel the Captain of all the
rabbits who left the warren Why don't you call
Bigwig the captain.
        Yours sincerely,
        Clayton age 8

When I next saw Clayton, at the end of March, he had received a postcard in reply:

Dear Clayton. Thank you for your letter. I can't answer your question in words but one day when you see for yourself why Hazel and not Bigwig was Chief Rabbit you'll understand a lot including the real point of the story. Best wishes. Yours Richard Adams.

Clayton says he does not understand this, but he later comments:

> *Clayton*   I should think Hazel was the captain because / um / Hazel thought of most of the plans / Fiver thought of going / Hazel asked all the others if they'd like to come. Fiver got Bigwig loose when he got caught in the snare . . .

And he continues to rehearse again various incidents in the book, trying to balance out the claims to leadership of the three rabbits. In doing this, he is discussing what the author himself describes as the central issue of the book.

Clayton's teacher (who had known him since he first came to school in the Infants and who made available to me the records she and another teacher had kept since then) felt that, through his questioning of the role of Hazel and Bigwig, Clayton was examining aspects of his own behaviour and personality. I saw only one side of Clayton in my conversations with him, and it is not my business to comment upon what I have not observed. Suffice to say that both his parents and his teachers experienced by turns his aggression and his sensitivity, and that Clayton knew he was someone who had fits of wild temper and moments of remorse and kindness towards others. This is not something he discussed with me – although perhaps he did, as his teacher felt, discuss it in talking about Fiver, Hazel and Bigwig, not resolving the problem, but holding it in balance. My own feeling is that he had already 'seen for himself why Hazel was Chief Rabbit', but was not quite ready to let go of the wish that it could be Bigwig.

Clayton finds, then, that fiction offers its own kind of knowledge. A story is still a book to be knowledgeable about in much the same way as he knows about farming; but what he comes to know through reading *Watership Down* is clearly something more than this. The difference is well shown in two sets of questions that Clayton posed. The first is this list of questions which he sent to me in a letter:

> How many rabbits come back from when they put the poison gas down the holes?
> How many rabbits did Bigwig get from General Woundwort?
> How many traps did the rabbits get caught in?

The second is a series that Clayton asked his teacher; in a recorded conversation:

> *Clayton*   How would you feel if you was one of the rabbits and Bigwig died?

T	I should feel very sad and I should miss him very much.
Clayton	If you were Pipkin who would you rather have / who would you rather have to protect you – Hazel or Bigwig?
T	*[long pause]* Mmm. Gosh that's difficult. In a way I'd want them both.
Clayton	Say Hazel had been injured / say Hazel was injured who would you have then?
T	If Hazel was injured?
Clayton	Mmm. Bigwig or any of the others.
T	Probably Bigwig I think because he was, as you say, he was a good fighter – but it would still be useful to have Hazel there I think, because even though he was injured he seemed to be very nice and I would perhaps still . . .
Clayton	. . . trust him.
T	Yes, trust him. Yes.
Clayton	What would you trust him for? Would you trust him to go to Nuthanger farm with the dog and the cat. Would you trust him to go there on his own?

This questioning of his teacher shows how 'articulate and specific' Clayton has become in his discussion of what he has read, and how he has mastered a mode of discourse for talking about fiction. But what is more important is that it shows Clayton exploring feeling rather than establishing fact: he seems to be realising that literature offers him a 'seeing for yourself' that is just as important to his sense of himself in the world as the expertise he has accrued about farming. L. M. Rosenblatt (1970) wrote: 'Literature provides a living-through, not simply knowledge about'; and Clayton, through that virtual experience and through his working out of that experience in various forms of talk and writing, approaches an understanding of what Richard Adams described to him as 'the real point'.

Clayton's completion of his teacher's sentence – 'trust him' – seems to me the most important moment in all his recorded work on *Watership Down*; and clearly the development of his reading, described here, owes much to his teacher, Hilary Minns. Her work with Clayton needs to be appreciated in the context of her relationship with him (of which 'trust', of course, is a part) and of the classroom community she and the children have established: these, teachers need to see for themselves and re-create in their own terms. But it is possible to extract from that work a list of Clayton's activities in association with *Watership Down*:

1. Showing other children his picture book and telling them the story.
2. Talking to another adult about the story on tape.
3. Talking to the teacher about the story on tape.
4. Making an advertisement for the film (in the form of a large cardboard folder).

5. Telling the story to the class in preparation for drama.
6. Acting out the story, playing the part of a character.
7. Asking questions: (a) in a letter to the author;
                     (b) in a letter to another adult;
                     (c) on tape to his teacher;
   (and getting answers).
8. At home, hearing the story read aloud, and reading to himself.

What is important about this list is not so much the individual items, which might well vary, given another child and another book, but its variety, so that there is the opportunity to experience the story in different ways and to work out that experience through a variety of forms. 'The giving of meaning,' writes Applebee (1978) 'is a slow contemplative process involving significant changes over relatively long periods of time'. It does seem that not only does a teacher need to provide time and space for a child to follow his interest, but also needs to be resourceful and responsive to what he does in order to maintain that interest, and allow that process to bring about change and not stagnate.

This, then, is how an 8-year-old read *Watership Down* – and I still say 'read'. I have already quoted twice from Clayton's last letter to me: but, to show both how Clayton has changed and remained the same, here is the letter in full rather than in half:

> Dear Mr Fry,
>   I am thanking you for your
> letter you sent me. I have started a
> new topic on farming. I have finished
> *Watership Down*. I read it on my own. I
> felt proud of myself.
>   from
>   Clayton.

4 Hazel

Hazel was 12 and in the first-year of her new secondary school during the period of my conversations with her. She was often away from school, and we met only twice, once in December, and again in March: other arrangements fell through.

Hazel was less of a volunteer for these conversations than the other young readers in this study. My first visit to the school coincided with one of her days' absence, so we had not met before our first taped conversation. Her teacher, Barbara Brown, who was also her form tutor, was especially interested in Hazel and concerned about her, and always had it in mind that Hazel might be one of the two people from her class that I would work with. It was Barbara who persuaded Hazel to talk with me; but after that first occasion, once she knew what I was doing and what it would involve, she agreed to help. Even though we only managed to meet once again, we kept in touch through Barbara and wrote to each other.

Hazel had a knowledge of books that no one else in her class possessed: the most important thing she knew was that reading was an experience that offered her support and friendship. Hazel was not bookish or academic: her career at school was already at risk through repeated absence. But it is my belief that there should be a continuity between the scholar's commitment to literature and Hazel's own belief in fiction: that work on literature must rest upon that first feeling for fiction that Hazel knew. That is what this chapter argues as it describes Hazel and her books.

Many of us have an image of the reader derived from an age of elegance that no longer exists: in his private room, surrounded by the shelves of his own collection, the reader holds the book, silent, engrossed. In this picture, the reader is a person of privilege, not only in the sense of what he owns, but that his separateness commands respect: he is not to be disturbed.

It is difficult to preserve this image now that times are changed.

George Steiner writes:

> The pace of being, the surrounding noise-levels, the competitive stimulus
> of alternative media of information and entertainment . . . militate against
> the compacted privacy, the investments of silence, required by serious
> reading.
>
> (Steiner, 1978, p. 10)

He does not relinquish his image of what he calls 'the classic act of
reading', but in order to retain it he has to accentuate the sense of
reading as a privileged act. 'Reading' has to be distinguished from
reading as a common pastime, and taught as an art where the participants
are 'allowed the critical space and freedom from competing noise in
which to practise their passion' (p. 202).

At the end of this chapter I want to argue against this patrician view of
reading, but for the moment I want to sympathise with Steiner and
acknowledge what I recognise in his anxiety about the book.

When teachers consider their pupils, they often regret their lack of
interest in books, in much the same way as Steiner observes 'the marked
decline in habits of solitary, exclusive reading' amongst undergraduates.
In Hazel's class, the children had no particular commitment to reading.
If they read at all, then it was just one activity amongst others (drawing,
watching television, football, listening to records) and not ranked highly.
Their teacher certainly regretted this and did much to try to counter it;
but it was only in Hazel that she recognised a kindred spirit – the same
'passion' perhaps. Hazel was a 'reader' in a sense that none of her
classmates were; and, although there was nothing privileged about her
reading places (a corner of the classroom, her bedroom shared with her
sister, the school lavatories at break), her commitment to reading
entailed something of that separateness and privacy of the reader in the
image with which I began.

What I have to say about Hazel is especially speculative. But the
question is this: why is Hazel a reader, and is there anything in the
answer to that which suggests why her classmates are not? Further, how
does this bear upon Steiner and the bleak assumptions that underlie his
question 'After the Book?'?

Here is Hazel telling a story about when she used to live in Lancashire.

Hazel   Well me mum and dad are divorced / me dad's down there / and
he's got the dog. We can't have it. He's my age now.
DF   Oh he's quite old then.
Hazel   Yes he's just gone eleven in September.
DF   That's old for a dog.
Hazel   Yeah we've had it since I were a baby and it were a pup. It's been
knocked down once.

DF   How did that happen?

Hazel   Well the dust / me mum and dad had gone out to work / and we'd
gone to school / and dustbinmen had been and left the back
door / the back gate open / and we usually leave / we left the back
door open for it to go out into the yard / the back yard / we didn't
have gardens / and it went in and the dustbinmen had been and
they'd / left the back gate open and it ran out / right down the
back / and into the road / and there were an old lady across
street / when it got knocked down she thought it were dead / she
took it in and put it in front of her fire on some blankets / and she
give it some milk . . .
. . . we saw that it were missing / when we / got home / and we
went looking for it / and she brought it across.

DF   And it was all right?

Hazel   Yeah.

DF   That was a bit lucky actually because he could have been

Hazel   Yeah / it were hurt / though. It were its back leg. It still limps a bit
now.

You can probably hear in this short extract Hazel's Lancashire accent.
Her way of speaking was 'strange' in her new school, and this was just
one of many things that caused her some unhappiness and told her that
this was not yet home. 'We usually leave / we left': the change of tense is
a tiny element in Hazel's adjustment to the change in her circumstances.
In telling her story, she has to adapt to a listener who does not know her
home and its routines; and she herself has to adapt to the knowledge that
much of what was close to her is now distant. Story-telling helps:
perforce it puts things into the past, but at the same time keeps them
close as a memory. To tell her story (which she did well), she has to sort
it out for someone else to follow, and in doing that she has to take
account of where she is now ('the back yard / we didn't have gardens'):
in story-telling, experience gradually settles into memory.

Here is the beginning of another story:

It was sunny and very hot. So the children's mother said to them
'Children it is a very warm day today so I thought that you might be able
to go for a picnic somewhere down by the woods.' The children jumped
up excited already and said 'Yes please mother we would like to go by
ourselves.' Lyn said 'I would like to go down by the stream in the big
field.' Their mother said 'Yes but don't go too far because you can get lost
easily.'

So the children ran upstairs and changed into shorts, tee shirt and
some sandals. They ran downstairs and John cried, 'mother can we have
some of that chocalate cake you bought yesterday and some biscuits'.
Their mother replied 'yes and I will make some sandwiches while you go
to the shop and buy a bottle of lemonade.'

Hazel wrote this in an examination for the first year: a competent piece, but not her own story and clearly not her own voice. She was asked to write about a favourite book (which she took as an exercise in re-telling), and chose a story by Enid Blyton, which she remembered reading when she was eight. (The children meet an elf who takes them to his tree-house and gives them presents of wooden wind-up toys.)

It would be interesting to know how this story has the power to remain in Hazel's mind so long, and why she chooses to recall it now; but Hazel cannot explain and I do not know. What remains is not just the story, but the way of telling the story: Hazel virtually assumes the voice of Blyton, and her re-creation of this story is markedly different from that about her dog in Lancashire.

Hazel has read much more than books by Enid Blyton, and in the school library can easily find and point to many books she knows. She can mention authors and titles, and also the names of series of books (such as the 'Antelope' series). She knows where to look in a book for information, and makes use of the flyleaf and the contents pages. When she goes into a library, when she chooses a book from a shelf, when she looks at an unfamiliar book that is offered to her, she is assured in what she does, and knowledgeable.

She reveals herself as an experienced reader in other ways, too. 'I'd read it too quick,' she says of one book we looked at; 'I'd like the story' (she had read the blurb), 'but more of the story and smaller print.' Print doesn't bother her: 'I don't look at the drawings when I read / just turn over and read.' She does not like books with 'big writing', but sometimes deliberately chooses such a book after she has finished a 'long book'. She has also learned patience as a reader: 'Some first pages are boring but they're interesting when you get further into a book.'

These comments – and Hazel's whole demeanour as a person talking about books – show her to be well able to direct her own reading, someone who is at home with books.

Books, too, help Hazel feel at home. She shares a room with one of her younger sisters, and often reads to her aloud; they read each other's books, and Hazel regularly reads books her sisters bring home from junior school. Reading is a family practice, a way all the children spend their time. Here, for example, is Hazel explaining why she went back to a book she had earlier given up:

> *Hazel*   Well my sister, she brought some books home and I didn't like them and I were getting bored cause they were all reading and so I decided to read that one again.

Stories can be comforters, and reading a book is like drawing the curtains or pulling the blankets around you: in unfamiliar surroundings, in changed circumstances, reading can make you feel the same again. And, private though it is, it brings you close to the people who are reading with you. In their new room, Hazel and her sister lie in bed, and each night read together.

'I can see one now,' said Hazel straight off, when I asked her to see whether there were any books in the pile on the table that interested her. In fact, she went on to inspect all the books, but eventually took with her the one she had first glanced at: *Little House in the Big Woods*. I think books often tug at us like this, no matter how coolly we seem to appraise and sample them. This title spoke more to Hazel than all the information she went on to find about the other books: in some way it is emblematic to her of feelings that concern her.

She read to page 57 and then stopped. Her explanation is 'I don't like people killing animals', but this is most likely derived from her teacher, who had also read the book, and who had said something very similar to me: besides, the killing of the hog, although it is told in detail, occupies only a few pages at the beginning of the story. Perhaps it is the way the story is told that is unfamiliar to her – a series of episodes, rather than a continuous narrative. However, page 57 is more than a third of the book, so Hazel has had time to become acquainted with this kind of telling.

My own feeling (and this is just guesswork) is that her reason for stopping is much the same as her reason for carrying on when she resumes the book a month later. The main character in the book is Pa, seen through the eyes of 6-year-old Laura:

> Laura looked at Pa, who was greasing his boots. His moustaches and his hair and his long brown beard were silky in the lamplight, and the colours of his plaid jacket were gay. He whistled cheerfully while he worked, and then he sang . . .
> . . . It was a warm night. The fire had gone to coals on the hearth, and Pa did not build it up. All around the little house, in the Big Woods, there were little sounds of falling snow, and from the eaves there was the drip. drip of the melting icicles.
>
> (*Little House in the Big Woods*, p. 69)

Time and again, the reader is made to sense the security of the family enclosed snugly in the small wooden house, despite the perils of wild creatures, rough weather, hard travelling; and Pa is the mainstay of this, with his ready competence, his cheerfulness, his story-telling and his fiddle-playing, and his obvious affection for his daughters. A feature of the book is when Pa tells the family a story, gathering them around him, and these occasions are often formalised in the text by the use of headings (such as 'Pa and the Story of the Bear in the Way'). Hazel said, 'The best bits I like is when / um / the father tells the stories about his travels going to town and trading his things and about his grandad when he was small.'

She finds it difficult to talk about Pa.

DF   Tell me a bit more about the father. Is he the sort of main character in the story?

Hazel   [A 7 second pause.] I don't know.

DF   What sort of father is he? Can you tell me a little bit about him as he is in the book?

Hazel   What / what do you mean / what like?

Her difficulty can be explained in several ways. First, my questions are put in difficult terms: she may well have talked easily about Pa in response to different questions. Secondly, it may be, as I think Applebee (1978) would argue, that Hazel is not yet able to respond in such terms and is only comfortable talking about a book when she is re-telling the story; sure enough, this conversation only gets under way when Hazel tells me one of Pa's stories. Thirdly, it may well be that Hazel finds it difficult to talk about Pa because of what has happened in her family and, thinking of this now, I wince at the obtuseness of those questions. I think what interested Hazel in the title *Little House in the Big Woods* is its suggestions of safety and threat, of domesticity and danger; and I suspect that the idealisation of family life, and particularly the character of Pa, is what at first makes it difficult for her to read on (she actually breaks off in the middle of one of Pa's stories), and then, later, what she finds valuable in continuing.

'I think', 'I suspect', I don't know – it may be that the book had much less significance for Hazel than I would like to think. I did not get to know her well, and perhaps some of the sentimentality of *Little House in the Big Woods* has rubbed off on me.

Around this time, Hazel read *Stranger in the Storm*, by Charles May, one of the Grasshopper books, which her sister borrowed from school. The story is about Adella, whose family move from the city into the country. It happens that Adella is left alone with Rhoda, cut off in her house during a snowstorm, while her parents are in town. The 'stranger' is an escaped slave, whom the girls help, even though they are afraid of him. But the story is primarily about the friendship between Adella and Rhoda: Adella finds that she likes Rhoda and comes to understand her, and she finds that people are frightened of what they have not previously experienced – Adella of the storm, Rhoda of the negro. Tom, the slave, continues his escape, and she knows she will never see him again, but she hopes she 'can hold on to Rhoda for a long long time' (p. 86).

Hazel read this – 87 pages – in four hours, and enjoyed it: again, I feel she has found something of herself in this book, has recognised what

Margaret Spencer calls her 'interior fiction', even though the setting of the story is very distant from her (Benton, 1980, p. 36).

The last time I saw Hazel she was reading Richard Parker's *Snatched*, in which the children of a diplomat are kidnapped, held under duress, threatened, in danger of their lives, and eventually escape. Here, the children are snatched from all that they know to be safe: the only adults are threatening, not protective; they have to fend for themselves, and they do.

Hazel wrote to me:

> When I read the book I read it in bed and my feet kept going sweaty. I really thought they was in danger and that they would never be let free. If I had been kidnapped with them I would be dreaming all sorts of things they would do to me. I liked the chapter best when the children got the iron bar and bumped into the man. From Hazel.

Snatched is a more demanding book than the others mentioned here. Apart from its length and the manner of its telling, it attempts to interest its readers in the tensions and rivalries between the children, and to explore certain moral aspects of their predicament: whether it is right, for example, to use the iron bar on Spider, and the shock of how they hurt him. Hazel does not seem much interested in this; what absorbs her is simply the situation, which again plays with the ideas of security and risk, of protection and threat, of dependence and independence. These might be expected to absorb all children, but they seem of particular importance to Hazel at this point in her life.

Hazel has a commitment to reading which has established itself in regular reading at home and regular weekly visits to the library at school. The books she reads are not exacting, and her interest in them is far from being intricate: yet we recognise in her a belief in books, a feeling for fiction – and this despite her lack of privilege in the shared room, the noisy school, the inner city far from the ivory tower.

We can guess at why books hold this place in Hazel's life. Somehow, through the influence of home and junior school, she has had the opportunity and the encouragement to read and to get to know about books. Somehow, her development as someone who tells stories and writes stories has interacted with her reading of stories, each informing and reinforcing the other, not just in kinds of competence, but in ways of thinking and feeling. Somehow, stories have come into her hands at important moments, so that she knows that the books she reads have the possibility of becoming part of her, just as we know that there are some books which are for ever associated with crucial moments in our lives. Somehow, she has come to be confident that books belong to her: reading is very much part of her view of herself; reading is something she does, rather than the concern of a more privileged or more clever class of people.

Steiner says 'we' must 'teach reading': and certainly when we try to be more precise about these 'somehows', we do need to look at what teachers do. Hazel has not been restricted to 'readers', but, from what can be gathered in conversation, has been given free access to many books and every encouragement to read as she likes. Teachers are familiar now with arguments about reading schemes, class libraries, story-telling, talking about books, and so on – recommendations for good practice which many schools have still to take up. Teachers at Hazel's new school, for example, were worried that, for all the advantages of Humanities and an integrated curriculum, there was little place for the writing of personal stories and the reading of personal choices of fiction; only recently had these teachers, who are unusually aware and thoughtful, but not specialist English teachers, begun to consider the deprivation of this. At the very least, where children are able to get at books, to hear stories, to tell stories, to have time and quiet made available for them to read stories, then it it likely that children, in that environment with that encouragement, will chance upon stories that will suddenly speak to them most powerfully – and at those moments reading becomes as important as friendship.

In this context I want to consider the comments of George Steiner (1978), in that I take him to be representative of an attitude towards books and the importance of reading. Hazel is no undergraduate, but there is, and should be, a continuity between our view of her reading and our view of our own reading, whatever our degree of specialism. Certainly views of literature in universities tend to wash back into the practice of teachers. Applebee (1977) concludes from research that children's responses are influenced by the teacher and the teaching method, which in turn is influenced by trends of literary criticism in the country. He (1978) reports a survey in which over half the 17-year-old students questioned chose as the most appropriate question to ask of a story, 'Is there anything in the story that has a hidden meaning?' – which says as much about their teachers as themselves. When Steiner elaborates upon what he means by 'teaching reading', we see this washback all too clearly:

> We shall have to teach it from the humblest level of rectitude, the parsing of a sentence, the grammatical diagnosis of a proposition, the scanning of a line of verse, through its many layers of performative means and referential assumption, all the way to that ideal of complete collaboration between writer and reader.
>
> (Steiner, 1978, p. 16)

There are some familiar debates lurking here for teachers of English.

Steiner makes a distinction between 'semi-attentive' reading and 'full reading'. The latter is explicitly claimed as the occupation of a minority, as though it were the pursuit of a specialist guild in which the master passes on his expertise to the apprentice: he speaks of 'the transmission of tensed delight before the word' from teacher to learner. Reading is 'full' in the sense of 'referential recognition, of grammatical confidence, of focused attention': it is 'a special skill'. Reading is difficult; and Steiner regrets that the availability of books and reading material has made reading too easy. Erasmus, he tells us, cried out at his good luck at finding a piece of a torn page in the mud: it would do us no harm to have to stoop too.

Perhaps we should not take all of this too seriously, but recognise that much of it arises out of the context of a particular problem in teaching undergraduates, a lack of familiarity with important texts. But we can also see here a move to make literature (for it is literature Steiner is discussing) a specialist preserve: the regret at the availability of books; the attempt to establish reading as a skill, with its hierarchy of subskills; the insistence upon the difficulty of it; the portrayal of the reader as a lone, intent scholar, sacrificing himself to his quest. Such exclusivity necessarily excludes: and what is restricted, what is difficult, what is dealt with only upon the terms of the teacher, is not attractive to young beginning readers.

Teachers have to think of stories as forms to be experienced, not to be expatiated upon. They have to let stories free, and let children play with them, not preserve them, or devise elaborate rules for their use. Hazel finds her own delight in books; it is not something she needs to be taught how to do, not something teachers 'transmit' to children. What teachers do transmit to children are attitudes towards reading. Do we believe Hazel's reading to be 'semi-attentive'? Is she not a 'serious' reader? What do we take 'full' reading to be? Has not, Steiner, in his 'tensed delight before the word', got something in common with Hazel's sweaty feet?

5 Karnail

I met Karnail on my second visit to his school: we had seen each other the first morning I spent with his tutor group, but he had not been one of the children to whom I had spoken at any length. From that first visit the class had some idea who I was and what I wanted to do, but it was really on the spur of the moment that Karnail volunteered to come and talk. After our first session, both he and I were happy to meet again. I saw Karnail on four occasions – in December, February, March and June. The conversations were usually about 45 minutes long, and we were able to use the nearby library in which to talk privately.

Karnail, aged 12, was in the first year of secondary school, and was coping well with his new work. He was not an experienced reader; indeed, he could be said not to have begun, even though he could read well enough not to be thought in need of extra support. In this chapter, I begin by establishing what stage Karnail is at in his reading, and then go on to show some of the difficulties that a young reader such as Karnail has in beginning to read a story. I then examine how, for Karnail, these difficulties were eased by his discovery that he could read Enid Blyton's Secret Seven books, and conclude by suggesting how Karnail's reading might move on from there.

Sometimes we borrow a book from a library that we imagine ourselves reading and yet never do: we are unable to find the time or we put the time that is available to less demanding uses; perhaps we can never quite summon up the will to begin, or, if we do, the effort to continue. No matter: we have no obligations to these books, and besides, we have to take them back.

We probably think of borrowing a book as being necessarily associated with the attempt to read it. But we can think of borrowing, especially from a library, as carrying no commitment other than returning what is borrowed. Being able to visit a library and to inspect any book one pleases is a pleasure in itself; and simply taking the book away is not only encouraged, but seems to win social approval.

The children in Karnail's class very much enjoyed going to the library, which was only seconds away from their classroom. They were allowed to change books in the registration time at the beginning of the day, and their teacher was always interested in what they brought back to the class. Karnail borrowed twenty or so books in his first half-term, and was known as someone who regularly used the library and felt at home there.

At junior school his choice of books was more tightly controlled. He worked at his Wide Range Reader (he reached the 'red label'), which was supplemented by other books labelled by colour and kept in cupboards outside the classroom. (It was 'like cheating', Karnail said, to choose a book with a label that was not your current colour.) Twice a week he was able to choose a book from a library trolley, but he did not remember much of these, except that some seemed too difficult.

Now, at secondary school, hundreds of books were accessible to him with every encouragement to feel free to choose and take home books – and Karnail made the most of this. He became an enthusiastic borrower of books.

Many of these books were about judo and football: here, techniques such as throwing in and skills such as marking were best explained by diagrams, drawings and photographs; the text was not redundant, but it was the illustrations which Karnail valued and 'read'. His other choices were not the children's novels that the library had a good supply of, but books that looked like the readers he had become used to at junior school: thin, paper-covered, with regular line drawings between chunks of text, and with titles such as 'The Trouble with Bruff' Data Book 8 and 'Doctor Thorne' Longman Supplementary Reader. Despite the freedom of choice Karnail now had, he seemed constrained by his previous experience of reading; and he did not pay much attention to these books other than looking at one or two pages, before taking them back to the library.

What guided his choice in fiction was more his assessment of a book as an object than as something to read: its size, its weight, its appearance, its status as a 'reader'. I do not think this made Karnail anxious; if anything, it served to relieve his anxiety. He was pleased because he had borrowed so many books, rather than embarrassed that he had not read one.

In reading, Karnail was still at first base; although certain preparations had been made, he had still to make the move. In the meantime, he had come across many books which later reappeared in other people's hands: 'Our teacher read this to us,' he said of a book I showed him, or 'Our football teacher read it to us once . . . I had it before him'. Some books were becoming familiar and could be recognised. His memory was also peopled with characters from stories that he had either heard about – from his father, his teacher, his friends, or the television – or had met in his 'readers': Jesus, Marco Polo, Samson, witches, Guru Nanak, the Sleeping Beauty, the Famous Five, the Sorcerer's Apprentice. Some of these he knew only vaguely, but well enough to recognise them when they reappeared in some other situation as the subject of another person's story-telling. In this way, Karnail, at first base, but receptive, had achieved some familiarity with fiction.

Apart from what the library had provided, he had from time to time taken in a further supply, but these, from a school book club, for example, or a book salvaged from those his teacher was throwing away, were at home unread. At home, too, were books his father borrowed from the city library, but these were in Punjabi, which Karnail could not read; and there were books his brother brought home from junior school, some of which looked promising, especially a collection of fairy tales, but which had to be returned by the end of each week. At best, Karnail had dipped into books, looked at opening pages, studied illustrations (some of which stayed in his mind); but these were brief forays, not the excursion itself.

George Craig (1976), from whom I have borrowed the notion of 'base', writes:

> Brief forays, like muscle flexings, sketch the possibility, even the imminence, of a new activity, but without committing the venturer to the venture: the base . . . is still non-reading.
>
> (Craig, 1976, p. 17)

Karnail prefers an activity such as football, which is much more recognisably *active*, not constrained, as reading is, by stillness, quiet and separateness. Craig draws attention to our vocabulary of struggle, risk and reluctance, by which we describe children's reading, and indeed our own, especially when we are thinking of reading as it happens, rather than the satisfaction which ultimately emerges – a satisfaction that a beginner knows little about. As we begin to read a text that is new to us, we are 'at risk': we are not completely in control of the situation, and we are uncertain not only of the pleasure that the text might hold, but of the very words in front of us – the 'language-practice', as Craig names it, that we are following for the first time. He likens our feelings to the heightened anxiety we experience when we meet a new person face-to-face. Sometimes our unease is momentary; we teeter imperceptibly as the ground rapidly establishes itself as familiar. But familiarity arises out of our past experience, and so becomes less likely, the more limited that experience is. The beginner, of course, is challenged more searchingly. Above all, it is the language of the book that confronts him. As Craig says, whatever qualities of imagination and sympathy we might call upon in our reading, what we must first show, in the early stages of the venture between the first base and the next, is 'whether we can come to terms with those words'. Karnail has been used to finding and handling books, and he has been a frequent listener to stories; but the page is silent and the print inert, until his reading activates it.

When Karnail inspects a book for the first time, he ignores the words. He relies entirely upon the pictures, often only the front cover, to give him, as he says, 'some idea of what happens'. His 'reading' of pictures is observant and exploratory: when he picks up a book, his attempt is, in his words, 'to make myself interested'. There is a description in Appendix B of his handling of *The House of Wings* (compared with the reactions of some of the other children in this study): Karnail is able to make himself interested in the picture, but he does not look inside the book or read the summary on the back cover. It may be that he just does not know about these things – how to find out about a book prior to reading it – but it seems that he feels that words only reiterate what the pictures tell and he is reluctant to deal with them. He scanned eight books in the same way, sometimes rejecting a book quickly where the front cover was unrevealing.

The Snowman by Raymond Briggs, a large-format story-book told entirely in pictures, was the ninth in the pile. When Hazel, who is in the same class, came to this book, she giggled and gently rejected it:

Hazel   (laughing) No.
DF   Why?
Hazel   It's just got pictures.

For Karnail, it is the one book he immediately opens and looks through. Surprised, a bit puzzled, he says, 'It's got no writing', and then with no prompting from me, begins to 'read it aloud':

Karnail   It's got no writing.
           This is a story with / picture story.
           The boy's asleep, wakes up, looks out of the window / gets his clothes on.
           Telling his mum something / like saying Can I build a snow-man / getting his boots on / cap / mother's looking out the window.
           First he's / made a little snowball / he's rolling it against the snow / each time he rolls it it gets bigger.

He continues until the end. The story-telling holds him, even though the bell rings and his friends come into the library to fetch him for football.

The story of *The Snowman* is as clear in its outline, and as friendly, as the snowman himself; and though, like the snowman, it has its own life and beckons 'Follow me', still the reader, like the boy, has a hand in its making. *'The Snowman'* has to be read – and offers more to the reader who is more observant – but it comes off the page with ease. Surely Karnail is not only pleased by the story, but *relieved*: relieved of words and relieved by their absence.

George Craig again:

> The reader's language practice is not simply aligned with the writer's: it has first to discover what that is and then, working from the signals generated by the discovery, accommodate the discovered practice.
>
> (Craig, 1976, p. 34)

Here are some examples of Karnail practising that: he is looking at the beginning of stories. (There was some artificiality in this exercise: for example, the extracts had been typed out so that they were no longer seen in the context of the whole book.)

This is the beginning of *The Golden Bird*, by Edith Brill:

> Once upon a time there lived in the great forest of the western plain a broom-maker called Babka. Her little wooden house stood in a clearing and was surrounded by a garden where sunflowers grew almost as tall as the chimney. The walls were made of logs dovetailed at the corners, and the space between the logs was filled with moss and clay. Every spring Babka painted this filling with a special blue paint to keep it watertight. The steep roof was covered with larch shingles overlapping each other like fish scales and these had become a silvery grey with age. Indeed, the little house was so old it had become as much a part of the forest as the trees.

Karnail states the gist of this:

Karnail   She lived on her own in the forest.
             Surrounded by a load of trees.
             Her house almost looked like the forest.

He leaves aside the detail of the description ('dovetailed' and 'larch shingles' are unfamiliar). The first thing the reader discovers in the story is the house, almost indistinguishable from the trees that surround it, and Karnail's first suggestion about the development of the story is that someone else might discover where Babka lives.

DF   Who might this someone be do you think?
Karnail   A prince.
DF   All right / a prince. Why do you say a prince?
Karnail   Might have gone out hunting.
DF   Oh yes that's a good idea. And what will the prince do?
Karnail   Take her away to his kingdom or something like that and marry her.

The problem is the next sentence of the story: 'Babka too was old; her face was brown and wrinkled.' Karnail, without too much difficulty, re-establishes Babka's eligibility: a witch has cast a spell that has 'made her old'. Why? Because she was jealous of Babka's youth and beauty. Karnail suggests that the prince breaks the spell by 'making her happy', and then has a second idea: the witch is destroyed by water. 'That's how she breaks the spell and makes her young.'

Karnail has enough experience of this kind of story to know what kinds of character and action are acceptable and likely. How does he know that it is a fairy tale?

> Karnail Because of / she / lives in a forest.
> DF   Yes but . . .
>   . . . what else makes it a fairy story? What other signs have you seen?
> Karnail The prince.
> DF   The prince all right / but you made up the prince.
> Karnail Oh yes.
> DF   He's not mentioned in those lines.
> Karnail Yes, like Sleeping Beauty.
> DF   Mmm, that's right.
>   Perhaps you can't tell / perhaps it's impossible to tell.
> Karnail The way the story / once upon a time.

Karnail sees that he has drawn upon his memory of Sleeping Beauty to help him read this story, but he sees, too, that there is some similarity between the two that has made him associate them: 'the way the story'.

The similarity does not simply lie in 'the way the story' begins: the tag 'once upon a time'. This is the beginning of *Little House in the Big Woods*, by Laura Ingalls Wilder:

> Once upon a time, sixty years ago, a little girl lived in the Big Woods of Wisconsin, in a little grey house made of logs.
>   The great dark trees of the Big Woods stood all around the house, and beyond them were other trees and beyond them were more trees. As far as a man could go to the north in a day, or a week, or a whole month, there was nothing but woods.

This is not a fairy tale.

> Karnail It sounds like a history.
> DF   It is a little bit yes. It happened about / er
> Karnail Sixty years ago.

The little house belongs in both stories: but the 'broom-maker called Babka' no more belongs in the 'woods of Wisconsin' than the 'little girl' belongs in the 'great forest of the western plain'. We can see that Laura Ingalls Wilder is deliberately drawing upon the wording and phrasing of the fairy tale; but we can hear the difference between 'Once upon a time there lived' and 'Once upon a time a little girl lived' – in fact, the second sounds false or coy to us. We can detect, too, a difference in subject: the fairy tale illuminates the clearing in the forest ('Her little wooden house stood in a clearing'), whereas the 'history' broods upon the immensity of the woods and the limits of the far distance ('The great dark trees of the Big Woods stood all around the house'). But we do not need to be explicit about these differences to recognise that they are there: we pick up, as Karnail puts it, the 'sound' or the 'way' of the story. Certainly Karnail is not explicit about the distinction he detects, but detect it he does: he recognises which language is being practised.

But here is the opening of another story – *The Battle of Bubble and Squeak* by Philippa Pearce:

> The middle of the night, and everyone in the house asleep.
> Everyone? Then what was that noise?
> Creak! and then, after a pause, Creak! And then, Creak! And then, Creak! As regular as clockwork – but was this just clockwork? Behind the creaking, the lesser sound of some delicate tool working on metal.
> The girls heard nothing. Amy Parker was so young that nothing ever disturbed her sleep. Peggy, too, slept soundly.
> Sid Parker, their brother, heard in his dreams.

One problem Karnail has with this is knowing who is in the story. 'Amy' is not a name he knows, and:

> *Karnail*   I don't know who Peggy is. I think it's a dog.

Another problem is his unfamiliarity with the way the story starts:

> *Karnail*   This ain't the beginning is it / of the story?
> *DF*   It is, yes.
> *Karnail*   Is it?
> *DF*   Mmm. / What makes you think it's not the beginning?
> *Karnail*   The middle of the night.
> *DF*   What would you expect to come before?
> *Karnail*   One day / one night.

He does not recognise the convention at work here, and is thrown by the abruptness of the opening and the compression of the syntax. An experienced reader sees that the author is playing with his expectations about the kind of story he is in: he probably suspects that his first guess is going to be proved wrong – in fact, it is not a burglar, but a gerbil (though, as the story shows, no less dramatic for that!). But Karnail requires to be more sure of his ground: this beginning bewilders him.

Karnail also read the beginning of *Walkabout*, by James Vance Marshall, again typed out on plain paper:

> It was silent and dark, and the children were afraid. They huddled together, their backs to an outcrop of rock. Far below them, in the bed of

the gully, a little stream flowed inland – soon to peter out in the vastness of the Australian desert. Above them the walls of the gully climbed smoothly to a moonless sky.

The little boy nestled more closely against his sister. He was trembling. She felt for his hand, and held it, very tightly.

'All right Peter,' she whispered. 'I'm here.'

Karnail   I don't think it tells you where they were. It says silent and dark / and the children were afraid / (. . .) / says their backs to an / outcrop of rocks.

DF   Yes. An outcrop is just a sort of pile of rock. Mmm. Where is this then do you think?

Karnail   Could be near the sea / where the rocks are. Someone might be following them.

DF   Mmm. And that's why they're afraid?

Karnail   Yes.

[26 second pause]
It says vastness of the Australian / dessert.

DF   Desert.

Karnail   Desert. *(laughs)*

DF   You know what a desert is do you?

Karnail   Yes.

DF   So it does tell you where they are. Well / they're in a desert.

Karnail   Don't know where the rocks come from.

DF   Because a desert's all sand?

Karnail   Yes.

Here, quite literally, Karnail is unsure of his ground: what kind of terrain is being described here? 'Outcrop', 'gully', 'peter' – these words are sayable, but they convey no picture; and he cannot reconcile what he knows of deserts with the mention of 'rocks' (and probably 'stream', too). The story does tell us where the children are, but not in terms that this particular reader can visualise. On the other hand, he quickly sympathises with the relationship of the brother and sister and their fear of the dark. He also predicts the development of the story: 'bushmen' will help the children; the children will be pleased to see them, but the bushmen will find the girl strange because of her size and appearance. In making these predictions, he is able to draw upon previous knowledge: a recent topic in Humanities had been the bushmen of the Kalahari Desert.

An experienced reader expects to find these uncertainties at the beginning of a new book and, in trying to make sense of these beginnings, he rapidly draws upon his previous experience, both of books and of life, to make associations and analogies, many of which he quickly rejects as irrelevant. Even so, the task is sometimes too great, and the book is closed. The difficulty is much greater for Karnail, partly because he has less reserves upon which to draw, and partly because it takes him longer to read a page: the longer it takes to obtain the information you need to make sense of what you are reading, the more effort it takes to be patient with the book. In these circumstances, how does a book stay open?

I do not believe that Karnail was reluctant to read; it was rather the books that resisted him. Sooner or later he would begin a book that was as companionable in words as *The Snowman* was in pictures; and for Karnail, as for millions of other readers, it happened with Enid Blyton. The actual title was *Well Done, Secret Seven*, and, after that, *Good Work, Secret Seven*.

Frank Smith writes:

> Children learn to read by reading. Therefore the only way to facilitate their learning to read is to make reading easy for them.
>
> (Smith, 1973, p. 195)

– and that is what Enid Blyton manages to do.

In the first place, the books are familiar as objects: thanks to successful marketing, wherever there are gathered two or three children's books, one of them is likely to be a Blyton. The books in the Secret Seven series are unmistakable, and each keeps to the same format: the distinctive cover (with the title, photo, the number of the adventure, and the author's personal signature), the list of contents (each of the many chapters with its own title), the drawings of the characters opposite the first page, and the number of pages (beginning on p. 7 and ending on p. 96). Further, even if a reader has not read one of the books before, he is likely to be familiar with the Secret Seven through television and through readings at school by his teacher – certainly Karnail was. As he studies the front cover of *Well Done, Secret Seven*, he is able to make suggestions about the story with ease:

Karnail	They're building a treehouse I think.
DF	Yes that is what they're doing. Yes.
Karnail	And one day someone might come and / they get into their treehouse . . .
	Tries to get up / a man / and they come back and all their treehouse is wrecked . . .
	They solve the mystery.
	. . . Someone might fall in the water / play hide and seek.

These suggestions are not wide of the mark, and even where they are not exact, they are in keeping with the *kind* of adventure that the Secret Seven enjoy. Karnail later discovered that the words on the back cover were a reliable statement about the story-line:

> A young visitor to their treehouse puts the Secret Seven on the trail of
> some thieves, but first of all they have to unravel some strange clues.

No mystification here – plainly put, but full of promise. Although
Karnail usually ignored the back cover of books, he began to make use
of this information in the Secret Seven series. In short, much of the
strangeness of a new book is diminished, and this is very reassuring and
encouraging to the beginning reader.

As he flicks through the book for the first time, he is further reassured
that, although the book is unmistakably a *book*, it is not unmanageably
long. The text is interspersed with drawings, and much of it is dialogue,
well spaced out. The chapters were just the right length for Karnail to
read one or two before going to sleep or going out to play football. Nor
was it difficult to remember where you were: Karnail found his place by
remembering the title of the chapter he had last read (the title is usually
a summary of what happens, for example, The Secret Seven Meet, Jeff
Tries to Remember). Enid Blyton also helps memories by frequently
recapitulating the last paragraph of the previous chapter in the first
paragraph of the new chapter, often repeating words and phrases. (For
example, 'This is fun,' said George. 'This is really *fun*! I bet nobody ever
had such fun making a treehouse before!' – the end of Chapter 4 called
'Making the Treehouse'. Chapter 5 is called 'Great Fun' and begins,
'All the Seven really enjoyed themselves making the treehouse.')

When the reading begins, there is no difficulty about the identity of
the characters. The Secret Seven are named and drawn on the first
page, and the dog Scamper is there, too. Although in some stories there
might be a problem in getting to know seven different leading characters,
in these stories it does not really matter. The reader gets to know them
en bloc: three are girls, and four are boys, one of whom, Peter, is the
leader; and that is all that needs to be known. Karnail cannot always
remember their names, or which of the seven was responsible for a
particular action, but this does not impede his understanding of the
story. Other characters are designated 'mother', 'policeman', 'thief',
'lorry driver', 'Jack's sister Susie', and their behaviour conforms to the
expectations of the Seven and the reader. Occasionally there is a doubt
about whether a character is good or bad, but the Seven resolve this by
observing appearance (for example, is the person 'dirty-looking'?) or the
person's treatment of animals – and they are proved right, of course.

Nor is there any difficulty about visualising the location of the story.
Places are described in brief: a wood is 'cool and shady', a street 'rather
wide, dirty with great warehouses on either side', Sid's Cafe 'a rather
dirty looking eating place'. In fact, the reader is not required to visualise
the details of a location, or to imagine that he is encountering a specific
place with its own regional or local atmosphere. He handles 'wood',

'farm', 'canal', 'railway station', 'High Street', and so on, in much the same way as a child arranges building blocks in making a toy town. His own knowledge of his own home territory is all he needs. As the action is not specifically taking place *there*, then the reader is free to imagine that it could be happening *here*.

As the reading continues, the reader finds the text pinned securely to his understanding by words that, as they recur, tack meaning into place without taxing memory. 'Where's my badge?' says Janet at the beginning of *Well Done, Secret Seven*, and then again, 'Where's my badge?' Mummy, after reminding Janet about keeping her drawers tidy, reminds the reader of the significance of the badge: 'What is it you want – your Secret Seven Badge?' In 36 lines, over the first one and a half pages, the word 'badge' occurs nine times: then 'biscuit tin' and 'orangeade' take over, succeeded by 'password', and so on. With such clear markings, no reader can go astray or become confused; the repetition gives him time to absorb any new element in the story, 'kitten', 'squirrel', 'book about ships', and so on. The same is true of the story as a whole, which is strung upon a repetitive line of 'fun', 'thrill', 'great idea', and, above all, 'adventure', constantly reminding the reader of the nature of the story and the satisfaction it provides.

Much of the story is in dialogue, and so comes to the reader directly through the voices of the Seven and the other characters. In fact, the narrative voice is very close to that of the children: at most points the text could be transposed into the first person from the third without any alteration to the wording other than a change in pronoun. It is almost as though the narrator were one of the Seven herself, writing a record that Peter could do just as well himself, if only there were time during the adventure. This makes easy reading: the reader, for example, is not required to make a distinction between the perceptions of the children and the observations of the narrator; there is no disparity of vision or irony of tone. The corollary of this is that the reader is as close to the Seven as the narrator: as the back cover says, 'The Secret Seven have thrilling adventures – read this book and take part in one of them'.

The 'adventures' are what Karnail enjoys, even though they are relatively unexciting: the Secret Seven never encounter a Blind Pew, or shoot an Israel Hands, or dig up skeletons on treasure islands. The 'action' is often no more than a children's game (playing Red Indians in the woods, for example, in *Secret Seven Adventure*) but the telling of the story is devoted to that action. It is not interrupted by description, explanation, past history, commentary, introspection, or any other kind of 'distraction'. The story is single-minded, not only in its narrative voice, but in its adherence to a continuous one-track narrative line.

There is a strong family resemblance between one adventure and the next, just as there is between one case of Sherlock Holmes and another, or between two predicaments resolved by Jeeves. The regular reader comes to recognise certain familiar, if not inevitable, elements in the story. At the beginning, for example, the Seven while away the time eating or playing games as they await the opportunity for a new adventure; similarly, Holmes takes cocaine or grows impatient with Watson as he awaits the step on the stair or the arrival of the telegram that begins a new case. At the end, Holmes graciously lets the police take the credit, trusting in Watson to record the true story; the Seven finally inform the police, accept their congratulations, and enjoy the reward. During the adventure, the children have their secret meetings, their negotiations with parents, their picnic feasts; they encounter some dirty-looking man, a kindly adult, another child, and some kind of animal, usually in distress; they have their sudden bright ideas, their false trails, and their moments in hiding. Readers of the Secret Seven share with all readers who have their favourite set of stories that enjoyment in the reliability of a plot that is organised around recurring elements. They know, too, the manner in which the story will be told: it will be a familiar practice. In time, 'Secret Seven' becomes, in George Craig's phrase, 'a reassuring label', even though 'it is still necessary to find out: disappointment, or worse, is always possible' (Craig, 1976, p. 34). Variations there are, but the Secret Seven do not disappoint: the theme remains the same. It is only when the reader changes that the stories suddenly become a disappointment, interesting only as reminders of a former time.

Just as a reader will persevere with a story that is 'difficult', if it seems worth the effort, so he will not bother with a story that is 'easy', if it does not engage his interest. Those characteristics of Blyton's story-telling that make her easy to read also make her boring and banal – to us. But Karnail was pleased by them; and, of course, the 'easiness' of the stories is dependent upon the pleasure they give.

The Secret Seven frequently make us wince: the way they speak, the way they eat, the way they conduct themselves, the way they relate to adults. They often seem pompous, bossy and prejudiced; and they are supported by indulgent adults, not only parents and policemen, but 'Cookie', 'Gardener' and friendly representatives of the working class, such as Larry at the garage. Naughtiness is as strange to them as poverty: they are scrupulous about good manners, and never dream of defying the code of conduct that their parents have passed on to them. Peter, in particular, often reminds the others of what Mummy and Daddy have said: do not carve on trees, do put on your coat if you are going outside, do have a proper respect for books, do not take more than seven ginger biscuits from the tin, and so on. Here are child characters who are a different breed from their young readers. Yet Karnail hardly seems to notice this, and when I questioned him about the Seven – how they were different from him – he found it hard to understand my drift.

To us, much of the writing seems, at best, quaint:

> 'Sardine sandwiches, honey sandwiches, a smashing cherry cake with cherries inside and on top, and an iced sponge cake. I say, Colin, your mother's a jolly good sort,' said Peter approvingly. 'Isn't she going to have it with us? I'd like to thank her.'
>
> 'No, she's had to go out to a committee meeting or something,' said Colin.
>
> *(Good Work, Secret Seven)*

Some mothers do go to committee meetings, of course, but do we have to read about their children, especially when they speak like this and eat such food? But probably the young reader is more interested in what he recognises here, the experience of sharing food with friends on your own and in makeshift conditions. In *Fun for the Secret Seven*, Janet says, 'I don't know why food tastes so nice when we all sit in the shed and talk. But it does' – and that rings true, even though so much of the children's speech has an alien sound. The young reader is more attuned to what he has in common with the Secret Seven than to what is different about them.

Above all, the Seven are *children*, and much of what they do is *childish*. The stories are just as much about the games they play as the adventures they have; the adventures grow out of the games. Half of *Well Done, Secret Seven* is about the making of a treehouse – 'This is enough adventure for me,' says Pam, 'Fancy having a treehouse like this!' – and about passing the time in the new secret place which sways in the wind like a ship. The society itself is a game and, in a different book, its solemnity and secrecy would give adults much covert amusement. As it is, Susie, Jack's sister, is scornful:

> 'Oh the grand Secret Seven!' said Susie . . . 'You've no idea how solemn their silly old meetings are. Passwords, badges, nobody else allowed in, oh, they think they're too grand for words.'
>
> *(Secret Seven Fireworks)*

But Susie is just another child who is, as Karnail says, 'jealous'. The reader is always on the side of the Seven, and never feels that their activities are something which children will in time grow out of. In these stories, young readers see their own play taken seriously and established as the norm. Whatever doubts they might have about the Seven as people, these have to be suspended in order to share their belief in the importance of play.

The 'adventures' themselves stay close to home, not only in that they happen in the locality, but that they take place against the routine of everyday life: rooms are tidied, meals are taken, and homework is done. The Seven do indeed act secretly, but never in defiance of their parents. Mummy and Daddy do occasionally demur, but are easily reassured. The Seven are able to reconcile two conflicting interests, the need to conform and the need to be independent: home and adventure.

The adventures are independent of adults in another sense: they are adventures that only the children can have. This is partly because the children are able to be in the right place at the right time, and, being there, are able not to attract attention simply because they are children – 'We can go snooping about without anyone suspecting us,' says Peter. The adventure often arises out of something they observe or someone they meet while they are playing, that is, out of their being children. Less positively, the adventure arises out of their lack of resources – they have to improvise, and exercise their ingenuity. They decide, for example, that they want to save a horse from being put down:

> Peter gave a heavy sigh. What a pity he wasn't grown up. He could then do as his father did – go to the bank and take out quite large sums of money.
>
> *(Fun for the Secret Seven)*

But, of course, Peter has much more 'fun' than father, despite his temporary regret. In fact, father has no sense of adventure, nor has mother. It is not so much a personal deficiency as a condition of their adulthood – and it is chiefly in this way that the adventures belong to the children. Mother, of course, is based at home, cooking, checking that everything is tidy, and making sure everyone is wrapped up warm:

> 'Mummy!' called Peter. 'Wait for us. We've got a wonderful tale to tell you! Do wait!'
> But his mother had gone scurrying back to the house, not liking the cold damp evening . . .
> . . . There came a knock at the front door.
> 'See who that is, Peter!' called his mother. 'I've got a cake in the oven I must look at.'
> Peter went to the door. A big policeman stood there.
>
> *(Good Work, Secret Seven)*

In *Well Done, Secret Seven*, the children tell Father about Jeff, the boy they have found in their treehouse; Jeff has told them about his uncle who is planning a robbery. The children believe Jeff; Father is sceptical, though kind. 'When you get a bit older,' he tells the children, 'you'll learn not to believe all the tales people tell you.' The children's faith in Jeff is justified, however, and *their* judgement of him vindicated. Father's knowledge of the world has let him down, and it is what the children have discovered that 'REALLY MATTERS' (p. 85).

In doubting Jeff, Father threatens the 'adventure' itself. If Father is right, the adventure is ended. It is threatened in much the same way when the Seven are unable to solve a clue or realise that they are following a false lead. In *Good Work, Secret Seven*, Susie deliberately tricks the Seven into believing that they have found an adventure, and by the time they realise they have been fooled, 30 pages have gone by. The stories often begin with the Seven in anticipation of an adventure, and the text is marked by remarks such as 'We haven't had any adventure or mystery or excitement for ages', or 'But the more you look for an adventure the further away it seems', or 'I wish something would happen. Can't we make up some kind of adventure just to go on with?' Above all, the stories are about the growth of an adventure: the waiting, the false starts, the sudden bursts of activity, the dead ends, the threats of foreclosure, and the successful conclusions.

'Mysteries don't grow on trees, nor do adventures', Jack explains at the beginning of *Good Work, Secret Seven*. 'They just happen all in a minute.' What Karnail admires about the Seven is that they are able to recognise an adventure when they see one, and that they seize the opportunity to participate in what is out of the ordinary.

DF	Would you want to be a member of the gang?
Karnail	Yes
DF	What's good about their gang? What do you like about them?
Karnail	I like the way they / get on to mysteries / adventures happen / I'd like to be like that.
DF	What's good about the way they get on to mysteries?
Karnail	When they like / they see someone and then they / so if we've seen someone we wouldn't think he's a sort of thief or something like that / but they just study on it and they find themselves in a mystery.

It is as though anyone could be involved in an adventure, if only they are alert and imaginative. The adventures of the Seven are closer to those of Sherlock Holmes (whom Peter mentions in *Well Done, Secret Seven*) than to Biggles or Bond; much of their time is spent discussing the case, and racking their brains. The word 'idea' is second only to 'adventure' in the Seven's vocabulary; what they most admire in each other is having ideas.

> Peter looked at Pam admiringly. 'That's a very good idea, Pam,' he said, 'I've sometimes thought that you're not as good a Secret Seven member as the others are, but now I know you are. That's a Very Good Idea.'
> *(Good Work, Secret Seven)*

It is what Karnail most admires, too. The adventure in *Good Work* begins when two thieves steal father's car, not realising that Peter and Janet are hiding in the back.

> DF   What do you think is their smartest thing in the story so far?
>
> Karnail The way that they was in the car / they ducked down and everything and they studied their / hands and / things like that and their hair.
>
> DF   . . . Is it because / what you're just saying is that they're particularly clever there?
>
> Karnail Yes. Because um / they're quite clever anyway because / um / if I was in the back of the car I wouldn't look at their hands or hair.
>
> DF   Yes. You'd just be / what would you be doing do you think?
>
> Karnail Mmm / just staying down and scared. *(Laughs)*
>
> DF   Yes that's true. They keep out of sight but they're also watching for clues.
>
> Karnail They notice the big collars and their coats and their hats.
>
> DF   And they notice the finger and they notice the / button.
>
> Karnail But / Peter thinks of another idea that he says / if we / if they did have a finger chopped off or something / they wouldn't / um / you know / they might have had their / um hands in their pockets when they go to Sid's Caff so they wouldn't have any / um like / ideas if they were the thieves. And he thinks about that and then / they say / and then / Colin has a guy in his shed and then Peter had that idea / and dresses up as a guy.

By the detail in which he discusses this (typical, by the way, of all his talk about the Secret Seven books), Karnail shows how the story has caught his interest. For, in these books, play temporarily becomes adventure, and the world becomes a place of incident, clues and suspects. It is also a place where children have status, where their interpretation of events holds sway, and where their actions have the power to straighten crookedness and end unhappiness. At the same time, the temporariness of an adventure allows the ordinary world to continue, where children are dependants of their parents and are free, simply, to play. This is an attractive make-believe; and, although to adult eyes the Seven often seem arrogant and prejudiced, to children they are attractive because of their ingenuity and goodness and, simply, because they are children.

The Secret Seven books give an inexperienced reader what Ronald Morris calls 'context support', in which 'the message of the text is already alive in some form or another in the mind of the reader' (Morris, 1973, p. 187). Morris suggests that a reader gradually needs less of this support as he becomes more experienced; but Karnail has more of this support when he reads his second Secret Seven book, and it continues to increase with each subsequent book in the series. His expectations of the text are confirmed not only from book to book, but from chapter to chapter and even from sentence to sentence. But, although he may not be moving forward, he is becoming more confident as a reader, and quicker too, without being any the less attentive to what is being said.

Yet it might be that his confidence in the Secret Seven series will make him prejudiced against other different books. Already there are signs that he is judging books against his expectation that they should conform to the Blyton mode. For example, when he studies the cover of Paula Fox's book *How Many Miles to Babylon?*, he suggests this:

> *Karnail*   There might be some / treasure / might be / near the island or something / they make a / voyage to travel there / bit like the Famous Five.

Or again, when he explains why he did not read more than a few pages of *Little House in the Big Woods*, he says this:

> *Karnail*   I thought it was going to be something like the Secret Seven. Someone comes in the woods.

Later, he rejects Robert Leeson's *The Demon Bike Rider*. 'I thought it was going to be an adventure,' he explained, but the first few pages seemed to let him down. Leeson's book might be expected to meet his requirements of 'children' and 'adventure', but Karnail is using these in the sense in which they apply in the Secret Seven books. Almost certainly, Karnail's next move, from a base that is Blyton to one that is non-Blyton, will be as difficult as his previous move from first base.

For the time being, Blyton serves him well. He wants reading to be part of his life, but he is not prepared to go as far as, for example, his younger brother. He described the difference between them:

> *Karnail*   I think he likes books. Whichever book he reads he sticks to them. In the end he finds out that they're all right.
> . . . He reads more than me.

'More' means more of a book, rather than 'more books'. Reading more is something Karnail accepts – 'I reckon it's good' – but not for himself, if it involves struggle – 'But I just don't find it interesting if I don't like it.' Blyton minimises the struggle. She also gives him access to another aspect of reading he has observed – the spell that a book can cast. He has seen children reading in school, oblivious of the activity around them:

> *Karnail*   Think they're in a dream world . . . because you forget every-thing about what's going on, and just read the book.

Reading is like dreaming in another way:

> *Karnail*   Say that / if I'm reading a book and that could happen tomor-row / like that.
> . . . Say if I'm dreaming of getting a bike tomorrow.
> *DF*   . . . It could come true, as it were?

Karnail Yes.
DF   What / to you or to them.
Karnail To me!

Could Karnail find himself in an 'adventure'?

The dream that the Seven enact is enjoyable, again for the time being. Our reading of stories is not really comparable to our dreaming of dreams, if only because we are not dreaming: we are awake, and we remember, consider, reflect. But there is something of the same wondering in each, this question of coming true. Dreams often take us to the edge, to the extreme, sometimes throw us over. George Craig wants us to think of reading itself as an 'adventure':

> We are endlessly preoccupied with boundaries. Early representations of these ('enemy lines', 'the edge of the forest') may be simple, but the play of our excitement is rather less so. By way of these named boundaries we are led into the pre-reflective exploration and provisional redrawing of others (fantasy/reality, tolerable/intolerable, I/he and, of course, reading/doing).
>
> (Craig, 1976, p. 34–5)

Blyton seems to represent the boundary between 'play' and 'adventure', between the world of the child and the life of the adult; but, in fact, she pulls the boundary line further back and steps into the circle to play with the Secret Seven. It is a redrawing of the lines according to her own rules, and there comes a time when the growing child turns away. Reading Blyton becomes no more of an adventure than taking a walk in the neighbourhood, round the block, and children revisit her only for old times' sake.

After my last talk with Karnail, he lent me his exercise book. One page is especially interesting: it suggests that Karnail knows his Blyton and will not for long be kept within her bounds.

> The two boys looked out of the window.
> 'Look John,' said Mark, 'There's that man again, you know, the one we saw yesterday.'
> 'Yes, I see,' said John. 'I wonder what he's doing in Mrs Smith's garden.'
> 'No good,' I shouted. 'Do you think we ought to call the police?'
> John thought for a few minutes. 'Perhaps we ought to but I don't want to make a mistake. It would make us look so silly. I know, let's go and see what he's doing. And then we can decide.'
> 'Too late,' said Mark smiling. 'Mrs Smith is here herself. She looks pleased to see him, so I should think it's all right.'
> 'Oh yes,' said John relieved. 'It must be all right.'

6 Sharon

Sharon was in the fifth year of her girls' comprehensive school, and would be taking her 'O' levels in the summer. As I explained in the introduction, Sharon saw her teacher, Gill Frith, after my first visit to her class, and volunteered to take part in the project. Sharon was partly acting on the suggestion that these conversations would be useful preparation for her English oral examination, and might possibly help her in thinking through possible assignments for her course work; but talk about books was something she enjoyed and she welcomed the opportunity to talk about herself as a reader.

I had five conversations with Sharon: on two occasions, the first in January, and again at the end of March, Joanne joined us; we also met for a second time in January, in March, and finally in May. The conversations usually lasted about 45 minutes.

The early conversations took place during Sharon's reading of *Shardik*: we agreed to meet so that we could discuss Sharon's responses to the book in the course of reading it, as well as when she had finished it. Unfortunately, she had to put the book to one side because of the pressure of other reading and revision for her exams, but she was still able to read enough for this chapter to attempt a description of what it is that Sharon does as she reads this particular text.

As the conversations progressed, Sharon became more and more interested in trying to put into words what it was she experienced as she read fiction. This chapter records her helpful observations.

'The reader becomes the book'; and, sometimes, even when her reading has ended, the reader does not immediately become herself again. 'The house was quiet and the world was calm' (Wallace Stevens, 1953), and sometimes remain so even though the story has stopped. Familiar surroundings defer to the book, and when they again nudge the reader, they momentarily seem strange. Not all readers know this.

Here is Sharon talking about *Jane Eyre*:

> *Sharon*   I can remember finishing that book and I don't think that I've ever felt like I felt before when I'd finished that book. It was / it was really funny. 'Cause I read it in the holidays . . . . I'd been reading it all day you know / and then I stopped / and / I went downstairs for a drink or something / and I can remember / thinking / Oh so and so has gone somewhere you know I can remember / thinking that something was happening in the book / you know and then it / then it suddenly just sort of clicked / and I realised Oh no it's not that's in the book I'm reading. It was really weird.

In several ways Sharon likes to keep books, and to let stories stay with her, (See Appendix C). She would sooner own books than borrow them; and she does not like lending books – perhaps because she knows how hard it is to give them back!

> *Sharon*   . . . And I prefer to buy my own books as well / so that I can have them there. I mean I'll get books out of the library but I prefer to have the / book for myself.
> *DF*   So that it really is your book.
> *Sharon*   Yes so that I can have it any time and just pick it up / when I want to read it again.

Taking a book back to a library 'just puts an end to it all'.

In another sense, too, the book stays with you longer the thicker it is. 'I like a book to last,' says Sharon. 'I really prefer a longer book, to get really into the book, its characters and that, than a short one.' When she wants a 'quick' read, she uses magazines: books are not for casual moments.

To choose a long book is another way of putting off the ending, although, of course, it is the ending that ever pulls the reader on. Indeed, the more the story absorbs the reader, the more she devours it, brings it nearer to its close; and that absorption makes the last breaking off all the more a moment of regret. Walter Benjamin (1977) suggests that as we read about the characters in a story we know in advance that we will 'share their experience of death', their actual death, or their figurative death – the end of the novel. Figuratively, too, the reader, by her consumption of the diminishing pages, has a part in that death, which, though it has its momentary sadness, also offers us some sort of comfort for our own lives. For some readers, then (with some books), it seems that finishing a novel operates upon our much more general sense of what it is to finish: both to bring to an end something that is not us and to bring to an end something that is us.

'Death' is a word that Sharon chose at the end of the last conversation I had with her: we had been talking again about the feeling of strangeness at the conclusion of a novel.

Sharon	It's like a death really isn't it? You've lost them and you can't really get in touch again.
DF	Yes, it is like a death but that's / if the book's your own you can always sort of
Sharon	Yes.
DF	resurrect it.
Sharon	But / perhaps that's like / like memories and photographs.
DF	But it's not quite the same is it when you read a book the second time.
Sharon	No it's never / never the same again.

It is comments such as this that show how attached Sharon can become to what she reads, and how, of all the children in this study, her possession of books is the most complete.

From endings to beginnings – and *Shardik*, which Sharon was just starting. As she is someone who reflects upon her experience of reading, and wonders about it, could she keep track of her experience of reading *this* book and help us to be more explicit about what it is a reader does?

Having already read and enjoyed *Watership Down* and *The Plague Dogs*, and wanting to read another novel by the same writer, she expected a resemblance between *Shardik* and her previous reading – and, at first sight, the book encourages this. But:

Sharon	I was / I can't / I couldn't get over how surprised I was that it wasn't like the others / because I knew they were all about animals / that *Watership Down* was about these rabbits and the route they took and so is the *Plague Dogs* and they were both modern types of book but that one is not. I think *Watership Down* was written about a real place as well.

Shardik is a giant bear, but it soon becomes clear that this is not an 'animal story': nor is it set in contemporary time (or, indeed, any specific historical period) or in a land that can be anything other than fictionally mapped. (Sharon had visited the Lake District, the setting for *The Plague Dogs*, and had drawn a map showing the route of the dogs' travels, etc.)

She does overcome her surprise, and adjusts. She describes the difference in terms of the way she feels as a reader and the way she has to behave as a reader:

Sharon	I think it's got a different style of reading to it. I mean / *Watership Down* / is just one of these / continuous books that you want to read and read to see what happens to the rabbits / but I think that one's different. You see it from a different point of view. You see it as if you're an outsider in this place.
DF	Yes / whereas *Watership Down* is . . .?
Sharon	You feel as if you're a rabbit / you know actually living with them.

Here, Sharon takes 'style' to mean the manner in which a novel asks to be read, and she equates 'reading' with the feeling of 'living with' the characters. The first chapters of *Shardik* tell how the bear escapes from the forest fire:

> Never before had it been forced to flight. For years past no living creature had stood against it. Now, with a kind of angry shame, it slunk on and on, stumbling over half-seen roots, tormented with thirst and desperate for a chance to turn and fight against this flickering enemy that nothing could dismay.
>
> *(Shardik*, p. 18)

'At first I thought,' said Sharon, 'because I'd read the other two, I thought it was going to be about this bear, and you were going to live with this bear.' But in Chapter 3 the first human character appears, and by Chapter 4 we have been taken to the town of Ortelga, ruled by the High Baron Bel-ka Trazet. The reader, probably expecting to undertake a journey with the bear similar to that of the rabbits in *Watership Down*, now has to think again.

> *Sharon*   It started off with the bear but now it's gone on to the people / and you're living with them . . . I think this one is going to be more centred on the people though / their civilisation.

This new expectation proves reliable, and 60 or so pages later Sharon is questioning the relevance of the first chapters, wondering what purpose they served.

Even though the beginning of *Shardik* seems to confirm what a reader might expect from 'the author of *Watership Down*' (as the blurb reminds us), it is difficult to read. By the end of the first paragraph of the earlier book we know where we are, and feel comfortable there: 'primroses . . . wood . . . fence . . . brambly ditch . . . rabbit holes . . . ragwort' and so on, ending –

'The gate led into the lane.'

Shardik begins in the 'great forest', a strange jungle peopled by exotic creatures: the naming of countryside plants – ragwort, dog's mercury, blue brook-lime – finds its parallel here in the naming of peccary, genet, barbet, armadillo, and so on: not simply the difference between a nature walk and a zoological expedition, but a difference of perspective, for the first engages us at ground level, amongst the rabbits, whereas the second estranges us in a vast profusion and confusion of flora and fauna. The first paragraph asks us to hear, rather than picture, the forest, working from the scuttlings upon its floor to the utmost reaches of the tallest trees, ending:

> Higher still, in the topmost tiers, where the sunlight fell upon the outer surface of the forest as upon the upper side of an expanse of green clouds,

the raucous gloom gave place to a silent brightness, the province of great
butterflies flitting across the sprays in a solitude where no eye admired
nor any eye caught the minute sounds made by those marvellous wings.

(*Shardik*, p. 15)

Here the syntax is more convoluted, the wording more dense, the prose
more rhetorical, appropriate, perhaps, to the statuesque forest it describes.
But this is hard 'to get into', as Sharon found, and continuing for several
pages without any break for dialogue (these creatures do not talk to each
other!), it demands considerable concentration from the reader. The
effort seems to be one of visualising the scene, of following the
movements of the animals. Sharon admired the description, but became
'a bit lost at one point'; and it is not until Chapter 3 in the scene where
the hunter is threatened by the leopard, that the story first prints itself
upon her attention. But, as an experienced reader, she persevered,
knowing that, in her words, 'you get back into a story if you keep on
reading'.

It is not simply the setting, and the way that setting is described, that
makes *Shardik*, as Sharon puts it, 'more mysterious'. The beginning of
Watership Down is literally signposted: the first chapter ends with the
words of the noticeboard that inform us of the truth of Fiver's dream.
But the story-line in *Shardik* is not so clearly indicated: 'You're just
given this bear', and its significance is slow to emerge. Sharon is
prepared to wait, and invests her attention:

> *Sharon*   I don't know what there is about it / but there's something
> that / keeps you there. I mean at the moment you don't know
> anything about this bear / and where it's come from and / what
> it's got to do with these people. But *[pause]* I think it's ever such
> a strange book.

That the bear does have something to do with these people becomes
clear with the behaviour of the hunter, Kelderek: he needs to tell his
story of his encounter with the bear, but will tell it only to the Tuginda,
the high priestess – not even the High Baron can command him in this.
Of course, there must be a connection: bear, hunter, town – our
knowledge of stories insists that there are links here, even if they be for
the moment secret. There are other indications, not obviously made, but
which Sharon notices as we follow the hunter through the town to the
Baron's building: the description of a table, for example, the corners of
which are in the likeness of a bear's head. Later, Sharon wonders about
the disfigurement of the Baron's face, which at first she supposed was a
battle scar, and which she is now 'beginning to think is something to do
with the bear'. Gradually we realise that the people believe in the legend
of Shardik, a giant bear sent by God, who will return one day, but it is
not until Chapter 9 that we learn the details of this 'myth', as Sharon
calls it.

There is always uncertainty about the bear. Is the bear simply what people make it, or does it really possess some sacred power? Is it a force for evil or for good or merely arbitrary in its actions? Are its actions the results of deliberate intervention or simply the workings of coincidence? Different readers will resolve this in different ways. My own feeling is that these questions are for ever left open, and that, during the course of the story, the issue sways one way and then another, but never closes – so that it 'plays', like a door upon its hinges. Sharon, by the end of Book One (roughly the first hundred pages), has come to a conclusion:

> *Sharon*   . . . the bear / I believe the bear is something sacred . . . I wasn't sure at first I thought it was just / er / like a fantasy just something for the story / but / now I think it is because of / um / certain things that have happened / what / oh there was one in the evening when that / there was a man going to warn the people in the city where they were coming to / and the bear killed him. That's what put me on the track of it . . .
> . . . He's sort of got these powers / that no other bear has got / and he's us . . . / I think he's going to use these powers to help the people.

But the bear also kills those who pray to him and seek to help him: he crushes the priestess Rantzay, 'letting her drop, limp as an old garment fallen from a line':

> . . . her tongue protruded and her head lay grotesquely upon her shoulder, like that of a hanged man. When Sheldra put one arm beneath her and tried to raise her a terrible crackling sound came from the broken body.
>
> (Shardik, p. 140)

This would seem to re-open the question of the nature of the bear, but Sharon reads it in such a way to make the killing consistent with her belief:

> *Sharon*   I think that was perhaps just an accident. In a way I think perhaps she was pleased to die that way / die under his powers instead of . . .

There is certainly some truth in this, but the episode is more ambiguous than Sharon allows: in one sense, the bear seems to embrace Rantzay, takes her to him (and Rantzay does seem to welcome this), but we also feel the savagery and pathos of her death, and the violence of the bear. Sharon, however, wants to 'believe in the bear', aligns herself with those characters who are 'on the side of the bear'; and, in reading the episode in this way, restricts the options in her response.

In an earlier episode Shardik kills an enemy messenger, but we cannot be sure whether this is by chance or by intent. Here, Sharon sees that this uncertainty is a deliberate strategy of the author:

Sharon   I think Richard Adams is trying to make you feel that / he
um / everything that happens is by accident / because of the way
that / he says well he's still looking for food and this is where the
food is.
. . . I / perhaps to / make the book more interesting because if
you do actually believe in this bear that / I believe in him
anyway / but if you did right from the beginning / I mean there'd
be no / no / um / question behind it on what was going to
happen.

I am suggesting that Sharon is trying to resolve this question too soon in
her reading of the book, and that she is unwilling to maintain in her
mind the uncertainty which she mentions here (and which I feel runs
throughout the novel). On the other hand, this may be one of those
provisional conclusions that one comes to during the progress of
reading, and which have to be revised in the light of future events.
However we take this response of Sharon's, what it does undoubtedly
show is her awareness of the teller behind the tale, and that 'keeping
track' of the tale itself is not simply a matter of following the events, but
of making decisions about their significance.

Just as there are uncertainties about the bear, so, too, are there about
Kelderek, the 'hero'. When he first appears in Chapter 3 he is referred
to as 'the hunter', and is not named until the beginning of the next
chapter: indeed, the signs are that he is a minor character in the story of
the bear, not that the novel will become as much his own story.

Sharon   At first when we went to the hunter you know you go from the
bear to the hunter / I thought that the hunter was just somebody
you know leading you into the story but now he's taking the story
on.
DF   Do you think Kelderek will stay in the story for the whole time?
Sharon   I think / I feel that he ought to stay in the story now / because
he's / started it off . . . I think in the end he's going to turn out
on top you know / because the way / they think he's some sort of
sign which I'm beginning to think perhaps he is myself / the way
he's a kind man and he plays with the children and keeps
himself to himself.

Sharon recognises, but cannot yet be sure of, a convention at work here:
just as the people of Ortelga see in the simple hunter (Kelderek Play-
with-the-Children) the humble figure chosen to be the instrument of
the bear, so Sharon sees the signs of a typical rags-to-riches character –
who eventually 'turns out on top'. But as the story moves on, Kelderek
seems to take a supporting role: far from taking the lead and initiating
action, he follows others.

Sharon   Um I thought / that he was / at first that was him that was
actually going to lead and be all his ideas but / it seems to be

> their ideas which he's / taken over like / perhaps not very intel-
> ligent and he's using other people's ideas.

The question of Kelderek turns not just on whether he will stay in the story, but whether he will preserve that simple goodness that first marked him out. Sharon becomes involved in the ethical issues that the treatment of the bear raises. The Baron Ta-Kominion, for example, sees that, if only Shardik can in some way be subdued and led, it will provide a powerful rallying point for the people; but this has to be squared with that faith in the bear which demands total subservience.

> *Sharon*   I don't think he really / believes in the bear. I think what / he just
> wants to use the bear to / win back the city / and he wants the
> bear to be there so that the people who do believe in the
> bear / will have the will to / fight.
> And it's his ideas / he's trying to / er / persuade Kelderek that he
> does believe in this bear / and so that Kelderek thinks he's doing
> the best thing.

Kelderek is persuaded to help drug the bear, and this seems to be a betrayal. The question now becomes one of belief in Kelderek, and of doubt about his role in the story.

> *Sharon*   Um I'm not so sure about / whereabouts he'll stay in the story.
> Before I thought he'd be the leader all the way through / but
> now that he's changed from this – from believing in the bear and
> then drugging the bear / I'm not so sure . . .

Again, her reading of *Watership Down* provided her with much more certainty.

> *DF*   You don't feel there is a sense in which (Bigwig) is the leader of
> the rabbits?
> *Sharon*   No. Think Hazel is the leader right the way through.
> *DF*   Right from the very beginning.
> *Sharon*   Yes.

But, even though Kelderek fails to match expectations as a 'leader', Sharon cannot ignore those parts of the story which strongly suggest his importance as a character. In Chapter 16 Kelderek follows the bear into the river, and Sharon – rightly I am sure – reads this as one of the crucial episodes so far.

> *Sharon*   Kelderek just jumps in after him without thinking. I think that
> showed some sort of / companionship between them something
> between them that / made him follow him.

Looking back, she sees a sequence of episodes which now signify a sense in which Kelderek, although not the conventional leader, is nevertheless the leading character.

Sharon   There's bits in the story where they're both together like no one
           else is with the bear. First of all when the bear saves his life / and
           then at the beginning do you find Kelderek sleeping beside
           him / and then he jumps in after him.

Kelderek stays with the bear, and so stays in the story; and, in fact,
because of his 'companionship' with Shardik he eventually does become
leader of the people, the new Baron.

Kelderek's position in the mind of the reader is confirmed as other
characters fall away: Rantzay is killed, Ta-Kominion dies in battle,
Melathys the priestess defects, the Baron disappears. It is a common
device, especially in novels of this length, that characters who have been
forgotten reappear later; but Sharon does not consider that possibility.
She presumes the Baron is dead or has fled, and she does not see any
importance in the flight of Melathys – 'I didn't attach anything to it'. She
prefers to accept the story as it happens, avoids predicting outcomes: she
makes a point, for example, of ignoring the page of contents, since the
chapter titles might reveal too much of what lies ahead. 'I mean you just
read it', she says 'just let it flow along'; and in the break between one
reading and another she reflects upon what has happened so far, rather
than looks ahead to what is likely to happen next.

Because a reappearance is a common device, the author here
disguises the possibility, and most readers would be surprised by later
developments. Probably Sharon is not sufficiently familiar with such
turns of plot; but certainly she under-rates the significance of the
defection of Melathys, even if we ignore the part she later plays.
Melathys is the first to 'betray' Shardik (it is Kelderek's word, though he
feels a sense of personal betrayal too); and it prefigures later events,
including, of course, Kelderek's own disloyalty. Similarly, because of
changes that have happened in the story, she questions the relevance of
the first two chapters, in which the bear flees from the forest fire: the fire
explains how the bear came to Ortelga, but is that something you really
need to know? Yet, of course, information is only one justification for the
inclusion of a detail or a passage: it clearly is important to our reading of
the book that what we see first, what we 'live with' to use Sharon's
phrase, is the bear, not the men. What Sharon also misses here is the
establishment of the motif of 'fire', just as she overlooks that of
'betrayal': but it may be that these are words that only resound in
retrospect, as the reading extends further into the book, and that when I
talked with her she had insufficient experience of the book behind her.

There is one last aspect of Sharon's reading of *Shardik* that I want to
mention, and that is the 'picturing' of what she reads. It is particularly
hard to be explicit about this; images seem as subsidiary, and yet as
fundamental, to our reading as do the words upon the page: when we

focus upon their formation, we cease to act as readers. We cannot both picture and reflect upon our picturing: our reading overrides, as it were, our attempt to think about how we are picturing. Yet it does seem that our understanding of what we read depends, in some way, upon the images we form. Iser (1978) suggests that our picturing makes present to us what otherwise lies merely upon the page, that it makes real what is not actually there and what we had not previously realised could be there and, indeed, what we know could not possibly be there – and on this rests our thinking as we read. It is the most obvious way readers use their imagination, and the most obvious way in which writer and reader co-operate. Iser writes:

> The image and the reading subject are indivisible ... the reader is absorbed into what he himself has been made to produce through the image; he cannot help being affected by his own production. The non-given or the absent enter into his presence, and he enters into theirs.
>
> (Iser, 1978, p. 140)

We become absorbed in a world that we help to create, and when we put the book down we experience, as Iser puts it, a kind of awakening – or, as Sharon put it, 'something clicked'.

'I can't picture it' is a reason readers often give for not getting on with a book. We have seen how much more difficult it is to picture the forest of *Shardik* than the fields of *Watership Down*; and in the previous chapter we saw Karnail unsure of his ground at the beginning of *Walkabout*. Sharon's teacher conducted an experiment in which she read aloud a short story, breaking off from time to time, and asking her pupils to jot down at each break what they were thinking and feeling: many of the pupils wrote about the pictures they had in their head. It seems there flicks upon the minds of some readers a rush of unconnected images, often incongruous, mostly fleeting, in an attempt to familiarise themselves with what they newly perceive; and that these images, certainly for these young readers, come from many sources in their memories, some of these private (as a picture from a nightmare, for example), and some of them easily recognised by others – in particular, pictures remembered from television and film. Readers vary in the extent to which they control this process, both in their ability to detect and discard what is inappropriate, and in their willingness to be controlled more by the text than their own freewheeling train of thought. But however intent the reader is upon the description in the text, clearly, in order to picture that, she draws upon her own remembered images, so that her perception of what she reads is a merging of word and memory – she not only draws upon, but is drawn upon by the inevitable association of ideas that the text provokes.

'Remembered images' suggest pictures akin to those in family albums: 'picturing' itself suggests images that are complete in detail, contained within a frame. Sharon says, 'In my mind I can see the forest with the bear coming tramping through it . . . I think I could draw what I saw.' Other readers 'see' what they read much less clearly: some might say that what they have in their head is not so much an image, but a sense of atmosphere, perhaps even an idea for a picture rather than the picture itself. The difference is partly explained by the manner in which the reader handles the text: Sharon seems deliberately to slow down her pace of reading, and to transfer the information she is given about the forest into a pictorial representation in her mind's eye. There is a kind of literalism in this (which Richard Adams seems to encourage by the detail of his scenic description), and it seems to involve Sharon in some unnecessary work: other readers, less committed than Sharon, but expecting the same kind of clarity in their picturing, are disappointed and give up the book. 'I can't picture it' is more a failure of the reader than the story, and one reason for the failure may be a misapprehension of what the process of picturing is. It is not equivalent to the task of the illustrator, who intersperses the text from time to time. It is more akin to the run of subtitles in a foreign film, especially where they are hard to make out; as though beneath the words there runs a subsketch, often faint, blurred, always partial, forever being revised. Our visualising for the most part is a half-seeing, a background of barely formed approximations which we can easily abandon, easily change, and upon which we can graft details and particulars when we need. If Sharon did draw what she saw, she would fix what is fluid, hold what is moving, focus what is blurred: but probably she could not draw it, and her thinking that she could is only an indication of her absorption in the world she imagines she pictures.

Ian Gregor (1980) suggests: 'It may be that the reader's vision is always incomplete, always partly in shadow', and shows that attempts to make this vision more exact, such as book covers that reproduce photographs from television adaptations, prove false to our experience of the book. On the other hand, such books, and books that arise from original films and television programmes, seem to offer something attractive to readers. Similarly, readers are often attracted by books that are set in places they know and where they have lived, or where they could visit if they wished – places that can be found on maps. If building images is, as Iser suggests, an essential part of the act of reading, then that act is made easier if some of those images are provided in advance: the reader works from what is familiar and her picturing begins from what is already in her memory. At one point in *Shardik*, Sharon has difficulty imagining the scene; here is part of Chapter 7, 'The Ledges':

> He was high up in some spacious, empty place, standing on a broad ledge of stone, its surface level but the texture so rough that he could feel the

grains and nodules under the soles of his feet. On either side were wooded slopes. The ledge stretched away to the left in a long, regular curve, a quarter-circle a stone's throw across, ending among banks of ivy and the trunks of trees. Immediately below it extended another similar ledge and below that fell away many more, resembling a giant staircase for giants or gods. The pitch was steep – steep enough for a fall to be dangerous . . .

(Shardik, p. 47)

Sharon's problem here is that she has no picture of her own, however approximate, to aid her:

> *Sharon*   . . . When I got to that bit / I hadn't got anything to relate it to you know. I hadn't seen anything / myself / any picture or anything . . .

This is one of those moments in reading where the words seem to resist the reader. Sharon likes to feel that she could draw what she visualises, and she recognises that the writer is expecting that kind of picturing (high up . . . on either side . . . away to the left . . . a stone's throw across . . . immediately below . . .). On this occasion she makes a virtue out of her difficulty, and equates it with the unfamiliarity of the characters in the story: 'I think it helped the story in a way because / they arrive at night and they wouldn't be able to see' – and indeed, although the passage accurately makes out the disposition of the woods and rocks, it is more that process of making out than the details themselves to which the reader needs to respond. All the reader needs here is some half-image of tree-tops and outcrops of rock, given point by the phrases 'staircase for giants' and 'a fall to be dangerous' – even though the terms of the description seem to require a fuller picture, and seem to require of us a much greater effort of attention; but we can be convinced by this detail of the reality of the scene without transferring the detail to our own picture of it. Is it that the experienced reader substitutes for 'I can't picture it' the realisation 'I don't need to picture it', and is content that his 'vision is always partly in shadow'?

Yet there are times when we do need to be more attentive to descriptions such as this. One simple reason is to avoid getting 'lost': when Kelderek arrives on the island of Quiso, we need to keep careful track of his journey or we lose our sense of his whereabouts and fail to understand his physical actions. One kind of picturing we do is the formation of mental maps, which are less exact than the 'maps' that illustrate the story (although they often assist us to get our bearings), but are fuller in that they are coloured by our imaginative awareness of the places they plot. Sometimes, too, less simply, we need to dwell upon a description not just because it 'puts us in the picture', but because it signifies other elements in the novel: metaphorically or emblematically it represents ideas important to the book as a whole, and our grasp of those ideas depends to some extent upon a visualisation of what is being described. At these moments, if our picturing is too literal, we miss the force of these images, and wonder about their relevance – as Sharon does when she looks back upon the beginning of *Shardik*.

When Sharon considers her image of the characters in the book, she realises that she has not given much thought to their appearance, and she makes a distinction between her picturing of places and her picturing of people. She remarks, 'I can imagine them being there but not their faces'. (The exception to this is the Baron, whose face is disfigured; but even here it is the idea of the scar that is imagined, rather than its precise description.) Iser explains the reason for this (and it is a point elaborated upon by Michael Irwin (1979)):

> Our mental images do not serve to make the character physically visible; their optical poverty is an indication of the fact that they illuminate the character, not as an object, but as a bearer of meaning. Even if we are given a detailed description of a character's appearance, we tend not to regard it as pure description, but try and conceive what is actually to be communicated through it.
>
> (Iser, 1978, p. 138)

Some of the same 'optical poverty' pertains to our images of scenes, but they need to be visually richer because they are *sights* above all else: we need to visualise them to sense their atmosphere; what they communicate is close to how they appear. But the presence of characters is different: we know them better than we can recognise them; familiar yet faceless. We see them in a way that we could not see them if we were actually to meet them, or when we see them embodied in dramatisations. Sharon has a vague picture of the Tuginda as someone in her thirties, whereas I thought of her as in her sixties. When we first meet her we are told that she is 45, something we had both ignored. But what matters is our sense of her as a 'bearer of meaning':

Sharon   I think she's / a very kind person she seems / you know the way
she / you know the Baron's / sort of / relies on his strength and
his weapons / I think she relies more on her intelligence.

The character is very much there in Sharon's imagination; but her image of her is visually faint, mentally clear.

It seems to me that the images we form as we read have the quality of the images we hold in our memory, and that, paradoxically, they have this quality even before they become remembered. Whatever the exact nature of the activity is, it seems to differ in nature and intensity from reader to reader, and again from book to book; and it seems to be a vital element in our characterisation of a reader – what her experience is as she reads, and how experienced she is at reading. If we could explain 'picturing' more exactly, then we might explain, too, that sense we have of having lived with the characters of a book, of being absorbed into a world which we seem to possess.

I want now to re-state these comments about Sharon's reading of *Shardik* in the more general form of descriptions of what Sharon does as she reads.

1.   She begins to read a book with expectations of what the experience of reading it will be; and these expectations, both general and particular, are based upon previous experience of reading.
2.   As she reads, she finds that she has to adapt or completely abandon some of these expectations.
3.   As she reads, she proceeds with a tacit awareness of the conventions of fiction. She reads it *as fiction*, and expects it to make sense as fiction. In a broad sense, she knows what usually happens in stories.
4.   Because she reads expecting it to make sense, she looks for connections and continuities: she is on the lookout for 'signs'. Where these are not immediately visible, she awaits further developments: what seems strange is made familiar by the acceptance of the further convention of 'mystery'.
5.   As she reads, and when she looks back at what she has read so far, she assumes and recognises that some episodes, some moments, some words even, are crucial; and that from these emerge sequences and patterns that shape the development of the story.
6.   She detects, also, that some details serve simply an informational purpose, whereas others, apart from what they tell us there and then, are indicative of possibilities in other areas of the story.
7.   As she moves further into the book, she begins to distinguish issues about the validity of actions and the motives of characters, which seem to invite the reader to take sides, but often remain ambivalent and are not necessarily to be conclusively settled.
8.   As she reads, she varies the pace of her reading as the demands upon her attention fluctuate.
9.   As she reads, she visualises in varying degrees what she reads. These images are sometimes highly defined, sometimes barely distinct. They help her become familiar with what she is reading, but also enable her to interpret that.

All this, and more, is 'reading'. It may be that, when we reflect upon our reading, we are able to consider these different operations; it may even be that, as we read, we are partly aware at times of one or more of them. Iser suggests that this awareness is particularly marked when our expectations of the text are contradicted or unfulfilled, where we encounter a discrepancy, or a 'blank', in the scheme of things we have been constructing from the text: at such times we sense an inadequacy in our reading, and so become aware of ourselves as 'readers'.

> [The reader] detaches himself from his own participation in the text and sees himself being guided from without. The ability to perceive oneself during the process of participation is an essential quality of the aesthetic experience; the observer finds himself in a strange, halfway position: he is involved, and he watches himself being involved.
>
> (Iser, 1978, p. 134)

Readers who 'see themselves' do not do so with reference to the kind of list I have made here. 'Reading' tends to resist such categorisation, as it does any attempt to consider it out of the context of its happening. 'The ability to perceive oneself' reveals itself in respect of specific contexts: what happens when this reader reaches this bit in this book. On the other hand, our sense of 'what happens', and the complexity of that, is sometimes helped by descriptions such as these, particularly when we are trying to perceive this process in someone else – the interest teachers might have, for example, in the reading of their pupils. Certainly it does seem that some such awareness is important in the development of the reader and her response to what she is reading; and that the corollary of this – seeing ourselves reading – is seeing the book as being written. 'The reader becomes the book' – yes; but the book only comes into being as the reader's reading interacts with the writer's writing. Perversely, in schools, and elsewhere, we often discuss books as though they only had writers.

Sharon is beginning to see her reading as being guided from without, and she is beginning to make observations about herself as a reader. I believe I recognise in my own reading what Iser calls 'the strange halfway position'; I do not believe that any of the readers in this study have experienced this. Sharon would argue that, as she reads, her involvement in the world of the book is complete: it is only in the spaces between reading that she considers her own reactions. Nor would she want her experience to be anything other. But it is beginning to be so. She is moving from the experience of reading which we recognise and remember as being peculiar to children to the experience which we would call adult – and which Iser partly characterises in his description of the 'halfway position'. But before taking this further, I want to summarise Sharon's comments on reading as experience – what it feels like to read a book, and what it feels like to have read a book.

Sharon says, 'You have to follow the book':

> *Sharon*   Writing your own story / um / what you want to happen can happen / and you've got some idea of what is going to happen

> next in your story / but when you're reading it's out of your
> control / anything could happen . . .
> . . . I mean you just read it / just let it flow along.

At first it seems disappointing that she should describe her reading in such passive terms; but in order to accept that anything could happen, she has to forgo her own wishes and expectations. She *is* in control – the reader can always close the book – but she surrenders that in favour of allowing the story to follow its own course. 'You just read it' is a more positive statement than it seems.

Sharon also wants to make the point that *as she reads*, she does not question what occurs. This is not because she believes that books are not to be discussed; in fact, discussion is what she values about her experience in school:

> *Sharon*   When I was young and before I started talking about books in
> school / I just used to read the book / and take it for what it
> was / what it said / but / you know / I don't read now and think of
> things beyond that / but when I finish the book I can / think
> about it and think what else the writer was trying to say.

She calls this 'piecing together', and, although she sees this as an important part of her experience as a reader, it happens once the book is finished. While the story is in progress, however, Sharon wants to follow it and not 'think of things beyond that', for to do so would be to detach herself from what she intends to be involved in – it would, as it were, break the spell.

For Sharon, reading is above all an imaginative experience, which invades and temporarily displaces one's present awareness.

> *Sharon*   The book is in your mind / you can imagine that you're some-
> where else . . .
> . . . It's like / as if you're there / but they can't see you and you can
> just see them.

Much of what Sharon says about this is reminiscent of the description by D. W. Harding. For example:

> It could be said that the reader of a novel is in the position of a ghost,
> watching unseen the behaviour of a group of people in whom he is deeply
> interested . . .
>
> (Harding, 1967, p. 12)

The 'ghost' watches so closely that he feels part of what is happening: as his own existence lies in shadow, he is given substance by the life he seems to share. Sharon would say, I think, that her ghost inhabits the life of a character for whom she feels, that her watching is through the eyes of that character:

Sharon   Like with / um / the first scene in *Jane Eyre* where she's sitting in
the window seat with the rain outside / you can actually feel the
cold window panes and the rain beating against them / and how
lonely she is / you know. You really feel sorry for her / feel it
yourself / I mean / you imagine yourself being there / being a
little girl sitting in the window seat.

Harding's terms 'onlooker' and 'spectator' stress the sense in which
the reader is detached from what she reads rather than the experience
that Sharon describes here. The spectatorship of the reader differs from
that of the man in the street in that the reader herself creates what she
seems to see: her watching is the result of her own imagining, and so
something of which she seems part. Sharon is more 'secret sharer' than
'ghost', and her watching is an active attempt to 'feel it yourself'.

Harding, of course, does not intend to deny that the reader responds
in this way: indeed, time and again he describes reading in ways that
Sharon or any reader would recognise and find helpful. What the use of
the term 'spectatorship' draws attention to is that the reader, for all her
sense of involvement, is never a participant. She cannot choose what she
sees, and she cannot intervene in the course of events. Sharon sees this
in her insistence that the story is there to be 'followed', and again, in this
snatch of conversation:

DF   But presumably you're doing more than just watching are you?
Sharon   Oh yes / I mean / you feel what they feel / and you / you only see
what they see / you know / you can't go off.

Sharon begins by agreeing that 'watching' does not adequately describe
the sense she has of sharing feelings with the characters, but then goes
on to acknowledge how limited her own role is. But these are limitations
the reader willingly accepts, for they make possible the 'consideration' of
experience that Harding describes. In characterising the reader as an
onlooker or a spectator, Harding shows how the reader, for all her sense
of involvement, is able to stand back from what has happened, and
reflect upon it.

Sharon has this to say about the effect of fiction upon her:

Sharon   I think it does change you definitely / because / um / you can see
another side to things . . .
. . . I don't know how to put my finger on it / you can see another
side to life . . .
. . . Um / there's just something else there all the time. It's
not / you know / you're not just living just / got something else. I
don't know how to put it . . .
. . . Like with *Jane Eyre* / you've lived with / in somebody else's
life / you haven't just lived in this age / you've lived before /
you've got yourself and then you've got bits of somebody else / in
your mind.

Sharon feels that the experience of reading a book adds to her experience in the more general sense: what happens in a book becomes something that happens in a reader, and then something that has happened to her. Iser explains this sense we have of living in the book by the nature of reading as an activity:

> In literature, where the reader is constantly feeding back reactions as he obtains new information, there is ... a continual process of realization, and so reading itself 'happens' like an event, in the sense that what we read takes on the character of an open-ended situation, at one and the same time concrete and yet fluid. The concreteness arises out of each new attitude we are forced to adopt toward the text, and the fluidity out of the fact that each new attitude bears the seeds of its own modification. Reading, then, is experienced as something which is happening – and happening is the hallmark of reality.
>
> (Iser, 1978, p. 68)

We often speak, as Harding does, of our reading being a kind of looking on; Sharon described herself as someone watching unseen. But Iser reminds us that what is happening in what we read happens in our minds, not before our eyes: our sense of its reality arises from the activity of our own imaginations – it is our 'realisation'. Here is Sharon, at the end of our last conversation:

> *Sharon*   I remember trying to read one but / you know / I just couldn't get into it. I just couldn't relate to the / to what was happening in the book. I couldn't imagine it myself.
> *DF*   Relate to what was happening / now /
> *Sharon*   By that I mean I couldn't sort of piece the pieces together and make it into something that I / you know / something that / um / was individual to me / how I saw the book / I couldn't make that for myself.

'You have to follow the book' still holds, but Sharon now makes explicit how active that is: it is something you make for yourself. In an earlier conversation, she described how she felt at the beginning of a book:

> *Sharon*   Perhaps it is sort of like / you're learning all over again / you're starting right from the beginning / um / I mean / you haven't had any thought of the book before except say if it was a follow-on from a book but / I mean you're starting and you're learning / and you're learning to get to know each of the characters in the book and the surroundings and where it's / you know / everything / start from scratch.

I find this idea of Sharon's a useful one and want to return to it at the end of this study: that reading a book is a form of learning. For Sharon this is the appeal of reading, something she finds attractive, not daunting, coming to know what is in the beginning unfamiliar:

> *Sharon*   I'm dying to get on to it*[Sons and Lovers]* . . . I want to find out
> what it's about / and I'll just pick it up and read the first line and
> after I read a few pages I'll know a bit more and then a few more
> and I'll know a bit more and / you know / by the time I get into
> the book I will know the characters and that / I'll be learning
> something new.

Sharon here talks of reading as though it is equivalent to visiting a new place or meeting new people: but she is probably not consciously aware of what these experiences also have in common, a substructure of expectations, conventions and strategies with which the 'newcomer' has to become acquainted. It is the 'learning' we saw as Sharon read *Shardik*, and it accrues from book to book, so that Sharon becomes experienced in the specific sense of how to read.

Sharon became more and more interested in the attempt to pin down her feeling as a reader. Her most careful formulation came in our last conversation:

> *DF*   Do you think books / books even if they're not obviously like life
> as you know it they still in a way reflect upon life as you know it
> or might know it / the fact that by reading them you / come to
> know life / understand things like / you know / what you said
> before / seeing the other side.
>
> *Sharon*   Yes I think you do.
> *[10 seconds pause]*
> Can't think of how to explain / it's like / um / experiencing some-
> thing but you haven't actually lived through it.

This virtual experience seems to be what we especially value about reading fiction. As we read, we re-enact what has happened as though we were there: re-create what has happened so that it becomes part of our own remembered experience. By the activity of our reading we give ourselves the sense of having 'lived through it', but because we have not actually done so, we are able to contemplate that experience in ways that are just not ordinarily possible in our lives. It seems to me that Sharon touches here upon the work of Susanne Langer (1953), and intuitively recognises what she has described, that our involvement through literature in virtual experience heightens our sense of ourselves as people who feel and consider and reflect; and that literature is continuous with our own lives not in that we recognise in some stories particulars of our own individual experiences, but in that we are able to feel, as we read, from beginning to end, what experience itself is like. The reader, said Sharon, is 'not just living', but has 'got something else'; reading is like 'learning all over again' – you 'start from scratch', and when you finish 'it's like a death'.

The reader 'is involved and watches himself being involved', and, in this sense, Iser extends 'spectatorship'. We speak of being lost in a story; but there is a kind of reading in which the reader is both lost and knows exactly where she is. When we become aware of ourselves as readers, then we become aware of fiction as art – and our involvement in what we read is altogether of a different order. I have tried to give some indication of what happens when Sharon reads, or, more important, what Sharon's perception of that process is. In their different ways, all the children in this study see themselves as readers, but Sharon is actually beginning to see the *process* of her reading and, in doing that, is becoming another kind of reader.

7   Joanne

Joanne was in the same class as Sharon – a fifth-year group in a girls' comprehensive school – but was not part of the same working group. I do not know why she decided to volunteer to help in this study; but she was someone who enjoyed conversation, and more than anyone else here Joanne took the opportunity to talk about and tell stories about experiences other than reading.

I met Joanne on five occasions: in January, February, twice in March, and May. Sharon joined us on the first occasion, and for the second conversation in March. The conversations lasted 45 minutes.

This chapter shows 15-year-old Joanne reading three very different books: James Herbert's *The Rats*, *Lord of the Flies*, and the Beatrix Potter stories. It suggests a possible pattern within this diversity of reading, and, in doing so, makes clear again that readers' responses to books are inseparable from their personal preoccupations at that time in their lives.

In Chapter 3 of *The Rats*, the monster rodents devour a pet dog and savage a 1-year-old baby. Here is an extract:

> The baby began to cry with horror as she saw her beloved playmate being hurt by the foul-smelling creatures.
>
> More rats came into the small kitchen but these were different. These were bigger, moving more cautiously, ignoring the violent struggle with the dog. They saw the crying baby, the bowl of dog food by her side. They slid forward, sniffing the air as they went. The food disappeared rapidly. They turned to the tiny figure.
>
> The dying dog seemed to sense the child's danger, and jumped away from its attackers, three rodents still clinging to its body. It fell upon one huge rat which was already biting into the baby's leg. Shane threw the monster high into the air with its last remaining strength and turned to face the others. The little dog lasted a few seconds more, fighting with frenzied desperation, and then its body was torn to pieces under a black, writhing mass.
>
> When Paula Blakely rushed into the room, she screamed in horror and utter panic. The scene didn't quite register in her brain. All she saw was a

room teeming with bestial, furry shapes, tearing at something bloody. And then a small white shape. A tiny hand quivering above the mass of black. 'Karen', she screamed.

(*The Rats*, p. 22)

In her retelling of this part of the story, Joanne shows how the scene has gained in gruesome detail since it was laid down in her memory:

Joanne   . . . She looks at the baby and she says Oh I'll just pop next door and / er / get some tea. So / the author makes you realise that she *has* only gone for two minutes but in those two minutes / the door of the cellar was slightly open and the / one rat / comes in to the kitchen out of the cellar and sits and stares at the baby and the baby's just a baby and she's sitting there playing with this puppy / you see / um / and the rat / first of all it bites at the / because the little baby is moving its fingers / bit the fingers and that made it snatchaway / and the puppy is trying to / um / fight this rat off because it's hurting the baby and he can see what's happening so then the rat turns to the puppy and then more of the rats come in when they've smelt the blood / more of the rats come in so / um / there's more and more coming in and the baby is / um / sort of torn apart / its arm is eaten chopped off / sounds horrid doesn't it / and um / then the mother comes back / that's two minutes and then the mother comes back and she sees them and she / runs in chonking on all these rats and they seem to ignore the mother / till it picks the baby up out of them eating / it's covered in blood / she picks up the baby and she runs out . . .

Despite the detail with which Joanne tells this (some of which she has herself supplied), she does so with no relish. She frequently hesitates, and speaks quietly; she prefaces the telling with an unnecessarily long preamble about cellars in London and making tea; and her comment 'sounds horrid doesn't it' is apologetic, not gleeful.

Joanne associates with the story in a way that makes its effects even more repulsive. Here she is telling of how the rats attack a drunk:

Joanne   . . . he / er / gradually tried to / um / stand up but he was pulled back down and another rat pulled him down from his shoulder and you can feel it happening you know / you can feel it jumping on to your shoulder and pulling you down again and his / his efforts trying to get up again / you can imagine yourself feeling really giddy / and these rats keep pulling you down and you're effort / effortlessly trying to get up again / and they're pulling you down yet again.

She gives this as an example of an earlier comment she made:

They are things that could really happen to you / and the way the author explains them / as if he has really had the experience . . .

But she credits the author with more skill than he has; the reader does as much to create the sense of 'things that could really happen', because that 'could' is a possibility she wants to dwell upon. Joanne, for example, deliberately associates her own experiences of baby-sitting with the previous episode, and thinks of herself in that kitchen with responsibility for the child: she begins, 'I suppose I love children and the one part was a little baby sitting on the kitchen floor.' No wonder that at times the book makes her shudder, that she can actually feel her response in physical sensations.

> *Joanne*   I came out of the hairdryer and put the book down and said Oh God I can't read any more. She [her mother] said Well I told you not to read it / but I went back to it the next day. It made me feel really ill / you know inside / it made me.

She understands why her mother does not approve of books like *The Rats*, and admits that they are 'not very nice' and 'a bit sick' (and, I think, recognises this as an understatement). Her mother, by the way, began *The Rats* and found that she had to finish it:

> *Joanne*   . . . and then she'll say to me 'Oh I wish you wouldn't read books like that'.

She does not accuse her mother, but sees her own experience of the book confirmed: that it is both repelling and compelling, that it is both a book you want to put down and cannot put down. What is unsettling about this, and, for example, makes it difficult to tell the story at ease, is not just the sadism of an accumulation of horrific episodes, but your own complicity in that sadism. 'Not very nice' is a quality not just of the story, but of the reader's personality, not just in the eyes of a parent or teacher, but in the reader's own self-awareness. 'I suppose I love children . . .' – Joanne clearly does (she is full of sympathetic and observant comments about the children she looks after), but how can she integrate that love with her reading, and telling, a story of a baby torn apart by rats?

   D. W. Harding suggests that stories such as this serve the purpose for the reader of 'fear formulation', and relates such a purpose to the 'suppose technique' of children's conversation. He goes on:

> Stories of terror and misfortune will appeal especially to the person who is only partially or superficially satisfied by conventional assurances that the world is really quite a safe and livable-in place. Secretly, perhaps only half consciously, many people doubt that, and it becomes a satisfaction to have the possibilities of terror and destruction brought into the open. Children want to read about dangers escaped and disasters survived. Older readers often prefer to contemplate the worst.
>
> (Harding, 1967, pp. 8–9)

That 'worst', I think, lies also in the nature of the reader, and becomes part of her contemplation. She is indeed, in Harding's terms, a 'willing spectator', but of such vile happenings that her watching becomes a form of unspeakable voyeurism, happenings that she actively 'wills', since the drive of the book, and hence its satisfaction, is its progressively horrific action: so that what is officially a disaster, such as the massacre by rats of a train-load of commuters on the underground, is a *tour de force*. Some of the vileness of the book rubs off on to its reader, and there may be something salutary, even necessary, in such an isolated experience. For some readers, but not Joanne, such books become an obsession at the expense of other experiences of reading and fiction: such literature far from enhances the life of a reader, and perhaps what was once the formulation of a fear becomes, in a succession of such reading, the expression of a desire.

Just as there must be other psychological reasons why stories such as *The Rats* appeal to young people, so there are more obvious explanations. *The Rats* was passed round the circle of Joanne's friends, in turn recommended to Joanne herself, as something faintly illicit: to read it is akin to accepting a 'dare'. The book has further appeal in that it is patently not 'educational' (Joanne's word), and does not win approval from those who monitor their reading; that it is 'not nice' perhaps makes it especially attractive to girls (especially in a girls' school). The book does not call upon any complex set of responses: either you laugh it off or it makes you feel ill. It has a primitive appeal, and yet, despite its lack of sophistication, it bestows a kind of worldliness upon its readers, as though braving its horrors and encountering the sexy bits is accomplishing an initiation rite, shedding another layer of innocence. There is also the fun of sharing with the group expressions of disgust, and of reading aloud selected pages to see how others react. Whatever it may offer the individual reader, it is also the experience of the group, and for a time becomes a 'craze' or a game that occupies them, one more thing they share as friends.

Given Joanne's unease about this book, and herself as reader of it, it is important that she can share her experience of it with her mother and her friends, and so see her own reactions to it in the perspective of theirs. What is also important here is that, for all her involvement in the book as a story of events that could really happen, Joanne reads it as *fiction*, and reads it as a particular kind of fiction, recognising the deployment of familiar devices. The most obvious example of this is the character called Harris (an art teacher), who gradually emerges as the one person to survive and finally to lead the successful counter-attack on the rats.

Joanne   There's been one man/Mr Harris his name is/who/er/
            Harris/no not Mr Harris/who has been/um/in the story all
            the way through/he's been the police's link and now he's the

> biochemist's link and the ratkiller's link etcetera and / er /
> because he's had experiences with the / with the rats and he's
> never been hurt / there's always somebody who's never been
> hurt but been close to it and has never been bitten . . .
> . . . but again Harris was always saved. He came into contact with
> them all the time / he'd always got a crowbar or something . . .

Characters who at first sight seem to be potential saviours perish,
despite their expertise:

> . . . there was the ratkiller man / the head of the whole lot / and
> he was / kneeling down / and one of the rats came out and bit his
> face out.

But Harris the amateur, the man in the street, survives, and becomes the
hero. Joanne recognises the convention at work here, and accepts it
without losing her awareness of its unlikelihood.

> . . . he was the hero you know / only everything all the other
> people had / um / died / he'd survived them all / you see. Which
> is / you get something like that in every book you read or
> every / um / film that you see on television. There's always
> somebody that survives.

There are other devices that Joanne accepts, but is not explicitly
critical of: the significance of 'cellar' ('Everything that's happened to
different people who have been killed they've all got cellars'); the placing
early in the story of the fact that bites and scratches are fatal ('kills them
in 24 hours'); the concoction of a final solution by the biochemists, the
doubts about its success, and the hero's part in that. To accept these the
reader has to accept what she is reading as fiction: conventions, which
often work to establish verisimilitude, here seem to serve the purpose of
clearly marking off the action from actuality. 'There's always somebody
that survives' is reassuring in two senses: it resolves satisfactorily that
play of the imagination, the technique of 'suppose', that the acceptance
of fictional devices makes possible, but it is also a recognition of those
devices, of substituting 'see here' for 'suppose', a way of getting out of
the book one was so much involved in.

There is one repeated device of the writer that Joanne does not
appreciate and is critical of. *The Rats* contradicts her expectations about
the introduction of characters into a story:

Joanne   Well in the beginning of a book it's usually / telling you the
characters that are in it introducing / um / the different characters
that are actually in the book.

DF   Yes.

Joanne   So you want to know all the characters that are in the book / so
you just carry on reading till

DF   And you want to know that fairly quickly so you
Joanne So you've got the gist of the book, yes.
        . . . I mean *The Rats* was hopeless at that sort of thing / it was just
        / um / the chapters were about completely different people that
        never came into it again / except the one man that followed all
        the way through the book.

Chapter 3, for example, begins (as many of the chapters do) with the name of a character new to the reader, in this case 'Karen Blakely', and then establishes for the reader something of the everyday life of Karen and her mother, as well as providing information about their past. We watch mother and child in the kitchen, playing with the dog, making tea, and we get to know about Karen's birth, the purchase of their house, husband Mike, the neighbours:

> Soon, when they'd saved enough money, they'd move out to Barking or Ilford, not too far from Mike's job at the garage, he was doing too well there to leave, but to a better class area, where you didn't have to keep a dog or a cat just to keep down the mice.
>   The whistle on the kettle began to shrill, interrupting her reverie. She turned it off and reached into the cupboard for the tea tin . . .
>
> (*The Rats*, p. 20)

Within two pages the baby and dog are dead, the mother savagely scratched, screaming down the street, and, as Joanne says, 'We never heard anything about them again, that was just it, they died'.

The author, James Herbert, subverts the usual conventions of realist fiction, plays one kind of story-telling off against another. He encourages the reader to form an attachment to a character by introducing that character in a manner which leads us to expect that character to have a leading role in the story, and then defies our expectations by immediately dispensing with what he seems to have created. Savagery thus intrudes upon normality more shockingly, and death is dealt out to people we seem to know, and thereby more cruelly. In fact, the procedure is so often repeated that the reader soon comes to expect an imminent attack of rats, and it is the quiet cups of tea that become abnormal. Some readers may well be alert to this procedure from the start (and would note wrily the reference to 'keeping the mice down'). The technique temporarily has the effect of contradicting an essential feature of such stories, that characterisation is redundant; but the interest that the writer creates in character is a fabrication, a meretricious device deployed to crude effect.

The device confuses Joanne: what is the point of Mrs Blakely's story, if she is not to remain in the book? But what she encounters here, in a sensational form, is an essential characteristic of narrative fiction and of a reader's relation to the text: that what we take to be the 'story' is an intermingling and an interacting, often competitively, of several stories, more or less complex: we are all tellers of our own stories, and characters in novels no less so, so that part of the reader's experience is in discerning what kind of story, and whose story, she is in. *The Rats* is trash; but from the practice of reading trash a reader can still derive experience of fiction applicable in later reading. It is often in popular fiction that we see most plainly the conventions that writers handle and readers learn, and where literary competence begins to be developed.

At the time of reading *The Rats*, Joanne's other particular interest in fiction was the stories of Beatrix Potter. She began to collect the books when she was 11 and they are associated in her mind with that period in her life, which, as she explains, was rather unhappy:

> *Joanne*   . . . I'd just started secondary school and I was really down you know / I didn't like this school at all / and / um / mum said she'd buy me a book / you see / because I never used to read unless mum read me a story / which she still does / stupid aren't I / and / um / she said / um / they were buying my brother something for his birthday present from / um / Toytown and I went up to the book part and I saw / which one did I first buy / oh crikey / um / Pigling Bland / that was the first one I bought. I wanted the one with the most writing in it . . .

She went on to collect the set, and also memorabilia and ornaments associated with the stories – for example, a special bookshelf and plaster models of the characters. Later, she became interested in the author, and had written to the publishers for information about her; she borrowed from me Margaret Lane's biography. She makes Beatrix Potter a hobby, and in various ways extends the imaginative world of the stories beyond her experience of reading them.

The stories are not as 'bland' as they are sometimes made out to be, and in their own way provide as much opportunity for 'fear formulation' as horror stories do for older readers: after all, Mr MacGregor really does mean to skin the Flopsy Bunnies and 'cut off their heads'. But what attracts older readers is the charm of the miniature world the stories present (and the miniature form in which they are cast), their domesticity and comfortableness, their virtues of quiet humour, delicacy of touch, and feeling precision. Nicholas Tucker (1981, pp. 62–63) suggests that the 'assurance of the familiar' that the books offer makes acceptable those stories that are about 'pursuit and the preyed upon':

> . . . partly clothed animal characters . . . mix the gentilities of polite conversation with offhand references to a more savage state.

That mix is probably what partly attracts Joanne, but for her the books are also associated with aspects of her own childhood, where stories serve as a solace and where the reading of stories aloud defines a homeliness and comfort of mind. I think Joanne is using fiction here in much the same way as 8-year-old Rachel and 12-year-old Hazel – as a way of recapturing the past and reassuring oneself in the present.

At first sight, it seems odd that the same reader finds satisfaction in two such very different imaginary worlds – that of Peter Rabbit and that of monster rats. But it is not difficult to see how the two complement each other: in general terms, we could speak of oppositions between naïvety and worldliness, sentimentality and sensationalism, security and threat, and so on. How they serve Joanne's particular purposes and meet her particular anxieties I did not enquire, but clearly both kinds of stories enable her to 'suppose' in ways that are valuable to her, different though the directions of those suppositions are.

Whereas Sharon had no clear memories of books from her childhood, and was not particularly interested in talking about these, Joanne several times mentioned stories she remembered, and did this with enjoyment. Unlike Sharon, too, she had no reservations about showing her interest in children's books. For example, 'I love fairy tales' – this was said in response to seeing *The Golden Bird*: she remembers reading 'Cinderella' and 'Snow White' over and over again. She reads to the children she baby-sits, and buys books for them, but, as she says, she still reads fairy tales herself and enjoys the books as much as the young children.

Unlike Sharon again, but in common with most other children, Joanne read lots of Enid Blyton. She remembers these with affection, one in particular:

> *Joanne*   When I went to junior school in the first year we'd have / um / the teacher reading to us right at the end of the day / and she read one story / I can't remember what it was called but I know it was by Enid Blyton / it was about five of them / and they escaped on to an island and left their mum and dad / they'd all escaped. It was / I can only really remember it vaguely but I'd love to read that again . . .
> . . . I was only seven but it's always stuck in my mind / I'll never forget it.

At home, apart from paperback Blytons for presents, she had her mother's own collection of Blyton hardbacks; books from our own parent's childhood have a special fascination. (*School Life at Bartrams* and *Little Meg's Children* are two I remember clearly from my own childhood, with their Sunday School presentation plates stuck inside the front cover.) Joanne's mother read these to her and, as she remembers here, helped her to hear how print tells a story:

> *Joanne*   ... when you're really young and your mum puts a book in front
> of you and it's got no pictures in it you're not interested. You
> know / the books like Enid Blyton wrote / well I was never
> interested in them because I couldn't picture it / if you know
> what I mean / but if mum read it to me then I could read
> it / um / understand it.

Obviously, listening to stories is an important reading experience (and
Joanne distinguishes here between reading as saying the words and
reading as understanding what the words say): important not only
because it helps the young reader to watch and hear the voice in the
print come alive, but because it frees her to concentrate upon picturing,
which as Joanne says, is the companion of understanding. Joanne's
mother still reads to her, as does her teacher at school; this is both
enjoyable and friendly, but also a support she still occasionally needs.

This brings us to the book that Joanne was reading in school, and
which she was writing about for her English literature folder (a GCE
examination by course work) – *Lord of the Flies*. The procedure was to
read set sections of the novel at home in preparation for work and
discussion in class. By this time Joanne was an experienced reader, but
still found the 'going over' in class very helpful, where the reading aloud
and exchange of views not only helped her develop ideas about the book,
but also to clear up some confusions about what had happened in the
story.

It is *Lord of the Flies*, by the way, that reminded Joanne of the
particular story by Enid Blyton. She sees the idea of 'island' as an
important image in her daydreaming and fantasising: Golding's is the
latest variation of the image that for Joanne was first worked by Blyton
when she was seven. It would be interesting to trace, though obviously
difficult to document, the development of such an image in the
imaginary life of an individual, and relate that to choice of books and
reading interests. Certainly Joanne felt there was such an image in her
own life, though we only catch a glimpse of it here.

'I think Jack and Ralph were naturally born leaders,' said Joanne, 'but
they both had different ways of expressing their leadership.'

> *Joanne*   ... Jack's way of leadership was trying to be / he was adven-
> turous / you know / and more interesting / only Jack wanted
> to / Ralph wanted to be / make the island more homely / more /
> you know / like civilisation. Jack just wanted to have a good
> time / and it / you know / overtook him.

The reader experiences this difference, as the novel several times makes
explicit, through the pull of a rival kind of story-telling, that of adventure
against that of realism. Joanne's sympathies are with Ralph, though she
recognises the appeal of Jack:

Joanne   Jack was stronger in the way that his leadership was more
exciting and more enjoyable and more interesting/he had
something/the tribal dances and everything. But Ralph/
Ralph's ideas were better. He/thought of/um/the shelters.
Making shells into bowls. And making a fire for any passing
ships . . .

Jack represents the values of the gang rather than the family: his appeal
is to instincts that are predatory, rather than what Joanne calls 'homely'.
Appearing to pull the story into his own kind of narrative adventure, he
drives it towards a realism Ralph and Piggy, and indeed Jack himself, did
not contemplate: a descent into primitivism.

Joanne   In my mind it was/um/normal boys/normal schoolboys/
turning into savages.

In the course of talking about the novel, Joanne took what at first
seemed a couple of diversions, but which in fact run parallel to what
most concerns her in the book. She referred to two items from her
recent television viewing: one a documentary programme about the
Rampton mental hospital, and the other a news item about an Italian
woman who had been locked away by her parents for 27 years. Both
offer possibilities for consideration similar to those presented by *Lord of
the Flies*. The Italian woman, said Joanne, 'was like a wild animal'; what
the film showed of the treatment of mental patients was 'horrible'. All
are examples of how human beings in certain circumstances lose their
humanness: in an essay Joanne wrote: 'Jack had completely given way to
his animal instincts. He was the leader of a pack of wild dogs . . . [Ralph
was] like a frightened animal hiding from the hunter, striving for
survival'. All are also examples of how inhumanely people can behave
towards others.

Joanne   I can't understand it/the way people/suppose it's because . . .
[4 seconds pause] I looked at it from my point of view/you
know/me being locked away.

She sympathises in this way with Piggy: 'he was an outcast, just a figure
of fun'. Piggy represents that quality of 'homeliness' that she finds so
important, so that when he is killed she feels 'the heart had been
snatched away and the life blood drained from the story'. The Beast is
there, both in what we do to others and what we ourselves can become.
But it is also there in our own contemplation of such things, in our
fascination with them. The reader feels the appeal of Jack's kind of
story; and the viewer says of a programme, as Joanne does, 'I just heard
about it today/it was horrible/it's on again tonight as well/I'd like to
have seen it.'
Joanne makes none of this explicit: these are my assumptions based

on what she mentions which, though different in kind, are in the same context. What she does make explicit is that *Lord of the Flies* is a boys' book – a book *about* boys, that is, not a book that only boys will enjoy reading. She cannot believe that what happens to the boys in the novel would have happened to girls.

> Joanne   . . . I don't think girls would have turned into savages and killing people / killing other girls. I really don't you know.
> . . . I think they'd have gone really bitchy catty but . . .
>
> DF   Was that something you were thinking of as you were reading? Were you sort of saying to youself.
>
> Joanne   No I didn't think of girls.
>
> DF   You just didn't think of them at all.
>
> Joanne   No. It was a boy's game / a boy's island / boys.

Joanne does imagine herself on the island in that predicament, but feels that the story would then have been very different.

> Joanne   That would be my ambition to go and live on an island . . .
> . . . I don't mean all on my own / I mean you know / with somebody else.
>
> DF   Some friends?
>
> Joanne   Mmm. And some little ones who are really babies, you know little babies.
>
> DF   And you have to look after them.
>
> Joanne   Yes.
>
> DF   Were you thinking of that as you were reading *Lord of the Flies*? I mean / they're stuck on an island aren't they?
>
> Joanne   Yes I was. The way they / er / ate the fruit off the trees and Ralph's idea was to / um / because all the little ones which / when they wanted to go to the toilet were just running up to the fruit trees / and he said Well you go into / go into the rock pool and when the tide comes in and out it'll / you know / clean the pool out. So his ideas were logical and sensible. He did have a responsible job you know . . .

Joanne associates with Ralph, partly because she is looking ahead to her own future: she plans to travel, and then get a job looking after children abroad. Ralph's responsibilities interest her, and the particular difficulties of his adventurous situation. But, of course, the novel does not develop in the way that Ralph would like. In an earlier chapter, I suggested that 8-year-old Rachel was 'bored' by *Treehorn* because it did not match her particular fantasy; but here, in Joanne's case, she continues to read. Does the story not touch upon her imagination in ways that she is not ready to be explicit about? Is the image of savagery that the novel presents not a deeply compelling one for her? And can we not see her talk about establishing the routines of home upon the island her way of countering her imaginative involvement, *as* she read, in the destruction of those routines and the creation of something dreadful? (In much the same way as Clayton counters the wonder of *The Snowman* with his own prosaic story-telling.)

The reader of *Pigling Bland*, *The Rats* and *Lord of the Flies* is the same person, even though her sense of herself as a reader may vary from text to text. *Lord of the Flies* raises questions about the nature of people, and her own nature, that also lay beneath the less demanding reading of the books Joanne chose herself, but of course it raises them in ways that are much more rewarding in terms of the experience they offer. I should say that at no time did Joanne make connections between these books: being of my making, these connections are clearly influenced by my need to make satisfying sense of the material I have. If the connections really are there, then it throws an additionally interesting light on the continuity, rather than the separateness, of home and school reading. Certainly the choice of *Lord of the Flies*, and the skilled way in which the teacher helped the class through the book, usefully redressed the effect of *The Rats*, and, albeit unwittingly in terms of this particular case, enabled Joanne further to explore feelings of importance to her.

In our last conversation, Joanne talked about her plans to travel abroad (especially America) before getting married. She felt she would leave this for a year or two, partly so that she could take a secretarial course as a further qualification, but also to have time 'to know a bit more about yourself and be more secure'. I think her reading, even though she is a casual reader in comparison to her friend Sharon, is an essential part of that 'knowing'.

What perhaps should have been mentioned at the beginning of this chapter is that Joanne much prefers films to books; I often felt that she would have liked our conversations to be about the films she had seen, rather than the books she had read, and often she turns the talk towards that preference.

Joanne feels that watching a film is a more moving experience than reading: 'I could never cry over a book', she says, as an example of what she means. Sharon, who joined in this conversation, cannot agree: 'If you're really involved with a book it can be just as moving or frightening as a television programme.' Again, whereas Sharon feels that films quickly fade from her memory, but books stay, Joanne says, 'A film lingers in my mind for ages and ages.'

What is so difficult here is to describe what this state of being 'really involved' is, and how the involvement of a reader of a book is different from that of a viewer of a film (and television, which raises questions separate from that of film, even when the 'programme' is itself a cinema film). There is a danger, too (especially in a study of this nature), of suggesting that involvement in film is of a lesser order than that in literature, that the limitation is in Joanne rather than Sharon, or, indeed, that there are limitations at all. Film offers us another opportunity to exercise what has been called our 'spectator role': it is itself a form of fiction and, although film offers a different kind of experience from the novel, it runs parallel to our reading, reflects upon it, not only in the choice of film or book we make, but in our understanding of our virtual experience through fiction.

But there is one obvious sense in which film is less demanding than the novel, and that is in the time it takes. Sharon enjoys the length of a book, and as she does not go out much (though she is by no means a recluse!) has the time, or perhaps makes the time, to devote to her reading. By contrast, even epic films are complete within a couple of hours or so. Reading makes demands on time in another way too:

> *Joanne*   Well I can't get/you can't read enough to get into the book
> before it's time to put it down again/you've got to go and do
> something you've been called or something [. . .] it's interrupted.

This is also a matter of space and privacy, which readers often have to make for themselves in difficult circumstances, but which the cinema guarantees as part of the experience it offers, so that 'getting into' a film is greatly assisted by the dimming of houselights and the preliminaries of rolling screen credits and music, as well as advance publicity and the billing of star names. V. F. Perkins, in *Film as Film*, writes:

> In the (ideally) comforting, self-forgetting darkness of the movie-house
> we attain faceless anonymity, a sort of public privacy, which effectively
> distances the real world and our actual circumstances . . . The erection of
> the shield (of darkness) seems to be the precondition of involvement.
> (Perkins, 1972, p. 134)

This 'public privacy' is again different from the solitariness of the reader, and it is especially so for Joanne, for whom film is part of 'going out' and then for discussion amongst friends. It is a corporate experience in a way that reading is not, unless a book is shared amongst friends, as was *The Rats*, or is read aloud. (There is, though, another kind of corporate experience pertaining to reading, and perhaps increasingly to film, in which the reader sees himself as part of a readership, one of a set of contemporaries who are admirers of an author's work, or one who joins those readers who have discovered or been initiated into classic texts.)

These 'preconditions of involvement' to some extent explain Joanne's preference for the cinema; but, of course, readers regularly accept them for the sake of the pleasure that is to come. An inexperienced reader – a reader who has not felt the pleasure of real involvement – will be deterred by these initial difficulties, which become a symptom of her inexperience. But Joanne is not a beginning reader. Her preference for film seems to be explained more by her sense of its importance: the film-goer has more status than the reader of books; films involve her in ways that seem more vital and significant.

As with many in her class, there is a close relationship between the films she watches and the books she reads. When the reading of the book follows the viewing of the film, then that enables the viewer/reader to extend the world of the film, to make it last longer: it brings to mind again the film itself, as the reader recognises a scene or detects something new, matching the images of the film against the text of the book; where the book is not the same as the film, it still perpetuates the story world of the film, and the remembered pictures help the reader 'get into' the new book. The images of the film help to create a visual reference point which the reader needs to construe the text. When the reading of the book precedes the viewing of the film, then the film brings the story to life: more experienced readers may feel critical of film versions of novels, but for Joanne it is the film that authenticates the book, confers realism upon it. She says of *Lord of the Flies*, 'I'd love to see the film to see if it's really like that', as though the film is there not only to confirm her own vision of the book, but the book itself. When she says, on another occasion, 'I've read the book and now I want to see the film', she is speaking of a routine she has established, a sequence to be completed, as though the experience of reading needs the experience of viewing to be entire.

Fiction on film does seem to have a special authenticity. Joanne says of an episode in *Carrie*: 'That frightened me that did when that happened, you know, when I saw that happen on the pictures it frightened me.' A film happening is seen to happen as it happens: 'when I saw that happen' testifies to the authority film has. But, at the same time, Joanne is under no illusion about its fictiveness, and that films have to be 'read' as fiction. Here she is talking about the documentary on the mental hospital mentioned earlier:

> *Joanne*   ... I don't mind seeing/films where people are tortured and because you know it's not really happening but when things like that happen I don't like it very much. You see it depends how you look at it I mean you could still watch it and look at it look as though it's not really happening/can't believe that it's happening.

She illustrates this further through two anecdotes which show her making a mistake in 'how you look at it'. The first is a memory from when she was 12 years old:

> *Joanne*   ... We've got the television where it's/well as you come downstairs you can see it and mum and dad have got the settee at

the back of it all so they can't see you so I sat on the stairs watching it till I didn't hear dad get up off the settee and walk out. I was sitting there watching this. I didn't realise / I thought it was just a film . . . I started crying.

She cries because what she took to be a film about an aircrash is in fact a news report, fact not fiction: 'the confusion of all these people lying and the plane' is a real happening. (The upset of this is intensified by being found out of bed, watching what she took to be an adult film.) The second is similar:

Joanne   This man was / he'd obviously been shot / and he was all covered in blood but I / I thought it was just / you know / a film.
DF   Because you'd come in half way through the.
Joanne   Yes / and I was saying to dad / Oh that sort of thing doesn't really happen does it and he said Oh yes that's true / and I couldn't watch any more.

This does seem to be a particular difficulty of television, where the conventions of television reporting either deprive events of their immediacy and hence, because of the nature of film, their actuality, or they render events 'live' in the idiom of film and thereby bestow upon them the quality of fiction. Only if we know how to look are we able to distinguish between what is happening and what seems to be happening. It is this 'knowing' that Joanne is talking about, and just as an experienced reader does not need to ask 'Is it true?', so the practised film-goer has learned to recognise those conventions by which film clearly marks itself off as fiction.

One of the interesting aspects of Perkins's book (1972) (however dated it might seem in the light of current film criticism and theory) is the way he holds film and fiction against each other. What he says here, for example, seems to derive from D. W. Harding's essays on the experience of reading:

We know that the experience (of a film) is unreal and in an important sense unimportant. We are freed from the responsibility of acting upon what we see and feel. . . . In the cinema we can observe our involvement while it is taking place. We enter the film situation but it remains separate from ourselves as our own dreams and experiences do not.
(Perkins, 1972, p. 140)

Although Joanne feels it is easier to become involved in a film than a book, I think she also feels it is possible to maintain this separation more easily in watching a film than in reading a book. This, anyway, is what I make of this extract of transcript where we are trying to discuss the ways in which watching what happens in a story is different from watching a film.

Joanne   Yes / I do try and put myself in the person who's being talked about / you know being written about . . . I shall / if if if it interests me I shall get myself / as / me being [the character] / and do what she did / go through what her life entailed.

DF   You can't do that though if you're watching a film / can you?
[*Note:* this said tentatively by me, not as a challenge, or as a statement of fact.]

Joanne   No I think you've just got to / no you can't / no. No you can't if you're just watching a film. You just take it / that it can't happen / it doesn't happen.

. . .

You can *stop* with a book and think about it / think about what's really happening / imagine what's happening.

What I take Joanne to be suggesting is this: yes, it is difficult to get into a book, to become interested in it, and my involvement is of a different kind from watching a film. I 'get myself', 'put myself' into the character in the book, and it is as though I have lived her life. When I watch a film I 'just take it', and all the time I know these are not real happenings, although I watch them as if they were. Because a film is continuous I do not elaborate upon it in my imagination: there is no break in the illusion, but also no break in my awareness of it as illusion. Whereas, in a book, I do stop, and in stopping I involve myself more in it, fantasising, making the book part of me, me part of the book. (The example of this she gives is how she incorporates her ambition of living on an island with her reading of *Lord of the Flies*.)

What we are getting at here is how the nature of a reader's involvement is different from that of the film viewer. I am suggesting that part of Joanne's preference for film is explained by her feeling that she can 'observe her own involvement' (in Perkins's phrase), that her involvement in film is marked by her sense of separateness from it. What Joanne is also saying is beginning to touch upon Susanne Langer's distinction between the kinds of virtual experience that film and fiction offer:

> Fiction is 'like' memory in that it is projected to compose a finished experiential form, a 'past' . . . Cinema is 'like' dream in the mode of its presentation: it creates a virtual present, an order of direct apparition.
>
> (Langer, 1953, p. 412)

So we need to think of 'immediacy' in film not disparagingly – that which makes film more accessible, 'easier' than fiction – but as the living essence of the experience it offers – what accounts for its feeling of authenticity, the nature of its illusion, the role of watcher in which it places its viewer, and the feeling of separateness it creates in the viewer who seems to view what she has herself made. For as Langer also says, 'it seems one's own creation, direct visionary experience, a dreamt reality'.

Perkins also speaks of the 'immediacy of film', but transfers this, too, to the facility of response he believes it makes possible. 'We are not aware of "reading" the image,' he writes (p. 138). But we need to distinguish between our awareness of the 'presentness' of film experience – 'I saw it happen' – and our making sense of that – 'how you look at it'. Joanne gives an amusing example of viewing the supporting film of the main feature, a film she had no previous knowledge of, her bewilderment at the kind of film she was witnessing, which in fact turns out to be a sex film. But for someone who 'knows', the film rapidly characterises itself through the conventions of the images it presents in its opening sequence. Viewing a film is indeed like reading.

And this is the point on which to end. I have only made a few suggestions, arising out of Joanne's interest, of ways in which the experiences of film and fiction differ and complement each other. But certainly they do reflect on each other. If teachers of literature can think of film and television not as rivals of fiction, but as allies, then readers may be encouraged to learn as much about reading through viewing as they do through reading itself.

8 Seeing Themselves as Readers

Even before we can read, we behave like readers. Very young children borrow books from libraries, go to bookshops, and number books amongst their possessions. They pick up their comics at the newsagents, choose from catalogues, and begin to make out the differences between timetables and maps and recipes and other things that they see their parents using. They handle and arrange books, turning over the pages which they cannot yet read, but which they recognise. They play at reading, accompanying their turning of pages with their own version of the story: perhaps they read aloud to toys, to an imaginary playgroup or an invisible friend. They play at writing, too, making 'books', or seeing their own words made into writing by adults and being read. They already know about books, naming titles, recognising books and series of books. And, of course, they attend to stories that are read to them, at home and elsewhere, feeling themselves to be part of a community that reads, and coming into the sure possession of what a story is and what a story does. They see themselves as readers, and we could say that unless they do so, and are encouraged to do so, they will not learn to read.

These activities are the social transactions that precede and surround the private act of reading itself. The young readers in this study have established their own routines and preferences amongst these activities, and their different personalities as readers are partly defined by them.

For Helen, seeing herself as a reader, and being seen to be a reader, confirms her sense of herself as someone becoming more independent and accomplished. That she owns books, and is able to tell other people about books, gives her some status, even authority, in the world. She values reading for much more than that, of course: her possession of *The Magic Finger* is not simply a matter of ownership. Part of her pleasure in being a reader, however, is that she is able to show that she's one.

Clayton's status as someone who knows about farming is supported by the books, pamphlets, brochures and magazines that he collects. They help him, too, to be like his father, but also an authority in his own right. *Watership Down* gives him a similar opportunity to establish an expertise:

in that respect, his move into fiction is an extension of what he already values in information books, especially as he makes it in the company of his father. His knowledge of the book gives him a standing in the class; at the same time, his thinking about the characters helps him to glimpse possibilities in leadership other than strength and aggression.

Karnail has an image of a reader – a person who reads all of a book and becomes lost in its story – and part of him wants to be like that. He regularly uses the library, taking and returning lots of books, knowing that this is one of the things that committed readers do. He is like a man who wants to believe and so attends regular religious ceremonies in the hope that what he has seen in others will become his experience, too. It is not so much that he wants others to see that he is someone who has books, but that having books encourages him in his own eyes to think of himself as a reader.

There is nothing sacred about books for Hazel – she treats them with respect, but does not particularly value them as objects. She is much more a borrower of books than a book-owner. In the company of books she is sociable, and through borrowing has accumulated a useful working knowledge of fiction (although this is not something she wants to display to others). It is enough to feel at ease and at home with books. Neither random in her choice nor 'choosey', she is open to a wide variety of stories, and enjoys them as one of her private pleasures.

Books hold Sharon, and, for her, books are to be held on to. A successful reading completely absorbs her, and she cannot part with the book afterwards. She shelves her books not as collector's items, but as keepsakes – reminders of past experiences, and of people, but also, once read and kept, reminders that these experiences can be relived and re-examined. Sharon likes talking about books, but, for her, reading itself is secluded and inward-looking. In any description of herself, Sharon would place great importance upon herself as a reader. In their different ways, so too would Hazel and Helen; but for Sharon the importance is that reading fiction has peopled her mind and extended her life, that without her experience of stories she would not be the person she is. That she is a reader means that she sees herself differently. For Sharon, her sense of herself as a reader is most closely integrated with her sense of herself as a person.

Joanne enjoys her reading, but where she and Sharon differ is that Joanne does not attach the same importance to reading as a very special private activity. Although all reading has an essential private element, Joanne's instinct is to share what she is reading. She enjoys the reading aloud that still goes on at school and at home, and the reading aloud that she does when baby-sitting. She likes the passing round of books amongst friends. What she is reading is another subject for conversation, and, in the classroom, she values the ongoing discussion of a book as it is read. Reading is just one of a number of activities that she enjoys – meeting friends, going baby-sitting, making clothes, watching television and, especially, going to the cinema. Even so, Joanne would consider herself poorer without her experience of books, and perhaps she senses that she is still in some ways an inexperienced reader, in that she has yet to feel that special involvement with a book that Sharon talks about and which, given the right circumstances, could occur for her. I feel, too, that for Joanne, as for all these young readers, books just as objects are valuable in their suggestiveness. Even without opening the pages, the differences between *The Rats* and *The Tale of Peter Rabbit* are not simply ones of design and production, but stand for different images a reader may have of herself. What we choose to read, or simply the books we choose to have in our possession, are indications of the ways we want to be seen and of the ways we see ourselves.

Parents and teachers do much to encourage the readerly behaviour that accompanies reading and which helps young people to think of themselves as readers. Teachers, however, find it harder to share in the reading and borrowing and buying of books that parents more easily do with their own children. It is difficult to surrender the role of supervisor in order to do the things the children are doing; but when teachers read their own books in silent reading times, take books out during library lessons, buy books from the school bookshop, and borrow books from children as well as lend them, then they demonstrate that they, too, are readers in just the way they would like their pupils to be.

Another problem for teachers is that school editions, though better value and sensibly bound, are not the books that children can find for themselves in shops and libraries. Even when they are, something in the stock cupboards seems to cling to them, and deprives them of their potential as individual possessions. To compensate for this, teachers have to spend some energy in encouraging children to have books to themselves: literally, through bookshops and class libraries, but also figuratively, through the imaginative quality of classroom experience. (Oddly enough, children often have in their own collections books from school, given away or sold very cheaply as old stock. Karnail had some of these, and was pleased to own them – they were now his.)

Books from school, and from libraries, do not have that special quality as objects that pertains to books that are personal purchases or gifts. Books that are presents are often from people we love, and when away from the family they remind us of home. The issuing of books by institutions – by teachers and librarians – is a transaction governed by obligations quite unlike those that accompany the lending and borrowing of books between individual people: the loan of a book is an act of trust and friendship, and a demonstration of a special interest in the recipient. Some of the books children most remember, even though they cannot keep them, are those lent to them by adults – teachers, too – from their personal collections.

I have written of the social transactions that surround reading, but I am aware also of the interactions between reading and feelings for other people, especially the family. Throughout these studies, we have glimpsed how the sharing of a story has brought members of a family together: Clayton and his father reading *Watership Down* each evening at home, Helen's mother reading her a favourite book as a reassurance in illness, Hazel and her sister reading together in their new room in a new home, Joanne and her mother sharing books and reading aloud, Sharon's mother lending books and buying books at jumble sales for her daughter, and Karnail admiring his younger brother and genuinely interested in him as a reader. The reading of stories is accompanied often by these feelings of friendship, comfort, encouragement and love.

Nor do teachers merely issue books. They know that the reading aloud of a story creates a special kind of attentiveness in their class-rooms, and that the reading or telling of a story is a helpful first step in building a relationship with and within a new class. They know as well that the provision of a regular quiet time for personal reading is a pleasure and relief for many pupils. Those teachers who take an interest in their pupils' reading – by keeping special lists of what they have read, or by exchanging views about books in conversation and writing, or by helping children to choose books, or by recommending books, or by bringing books into the classroom with particular children in mind – are at the same time showing their interest in their pupils as people.

Books can also be the agents of threat between children and adults: reading can give rise to feelings of disappointment, resentment and rage. Our image of ourselves as readers is susceptible to the same blows that strike the other faces of our personality; indeed, we see ourselves as readers through the same eyes with which we see ourselves as parents, children, brothers, sisters, friends, and all the personal roles we fill. For the young people in this study, reading seems to interact positively with feelings for others, and in this they are helped to feel secure in themselves both as readers and people.

As readers, children see themselves, and see for themselves; and as readers of fiction this 'seeing' is a special kind of learning.

There is a sense in which readers learn from stories that is close to our traditional idea of learning as the acquisition of information. For very young readers, what is seen in picture books often precedes the actual sight of things in life; and this pre-viewing of actuality remains some part of our interest in fiction. We also value in stories information about past life, or life we are unlikely to encounter. A novel that is well researched will impart to its readers much of interest about other walks of life, other countries, or other times: often one of the attractions of a novel is its 'inside' information, its revelation of the interior workings of institutions and professions we only know from the outside. Children are often interested in books that add to their own specialist store of information: we have seen Clayton taking in facts from *Watership Down* about rabbits and the countryside. Realistic detail confirms a story in our belief, and the story absorbs and transforms the information upon which it depends so that it is breathed in as we read.

We also learn from stories when they run parallel to our own lives, or when they serve a predictive function in advance of pending experience. Older readers are often pleased by novels that recapture their sense of how life was; but for younger readers, their lives still very much before them, novels are often valuable for their insights into present and future experience, how it is and might be. This is not simply a matter of information or advice, but an aid to that esential picturing we all do in advance of new experience, when we run through in our imaginations what it might be like. One of the books that Joanne enjoyed was Valerie Avery's *London Morning*, dated in many respects, but close enough to Joanne's experience for her to effect a match with its heroine, recognise happenings and feelings, and ponder upon what might be in store for herself.

There are times when our need for information is uppermost in our motives as readers. There are times, too, especially in schools, when information books pretend to be stories, and when stories are thought only good for the information they contain. The readers in this study hardly comment at all upon this kind of learning as one of their satisfactions from stories. Not surprisingly, for if we look for facts in stories, then we do not read them as fiction, and it is as readers of fiction that these young readers see themselves, and value their reading.

Harold Rosen writes that, in fictional narratives, 'the "facts" are re-organised so that what happened becomes what might happen; in this way fiction encompasses and extends the *possibilities* of human experience' (Rosen, 1984). He agrees with D. W. Harding that fiction has much in common with the many kinds of stories we daily tell each other. As Harding (1967) says, 'all these forms of narrative invite us to be onlookers joining in the evaluation of some possibility of experience'. In this way, too, we learn from stories.

We are especially interested to consider what we have read because of our sense of the story belonging to us. Our role as 'onlooker' is more active than the word suggests: as readers, we have found out for ourselves what has happened – indeed, have made it happen by the imaginative activity of our reading. At the same time, we have found ourselves in the story.

There seem to be two main ways in which readers see themselves in books; they are characterised in a conversation between Sharon and Joanne. Joanne says of the girl in *London Morning*:

Joanne   I was somebody watching her doing what she was doing, you know, doing / the actual things she did . . .
. . . walking behind her, standing right behind her.
. . . You don't see yourself there / you're like a shadow.

Sharon says of *Jane Eyre*:

Sharon   . . . you imagine yourself being there, being a little girl sitting in the window seat . . .
. . . I'm saying that I actually feel that I am the person.

These seem to be descriptions of two different kinds of readers, but, as Sharon says, they are rather modes of reading, which vary within a book and between books:

Sharon   In certain parts in some books you can imagine you're the person but in others you're *with* them but not actually them themselves.

Our involvement changes, responding to the varying invitations of the text: our picturing as we read puts us there in the story, and unless we find ourselves there, the story passes us by.

Novels, in retrospect, present us with kinds of case history. Our discussion of them is not touched by the urgency that would be appropriate to factual documents referring to people's actual predicaments, but it does have the urgency born of our sense of involvement – this is part of our remembered experience, we have seen ourselves in this. As Sharon said, 'You've got yourself and then you've got bits of somebody else, in your mind'; and we want to know how we feel about this somebody else. We can call this 'evaluation', but perhaps it is too judicious a word.

The evaluation is formative as well as summative. Whatever Sharon, for example, feels about Kelderek at the end of *Shardik*, her reading has taken her through shifts of opinion: in finding out what happens, she has to make provisional judgements about the nature of some of those happenings – is this, for instance, a betrayal? Joanne's reflections at the end of *Lord of the Flies* are made in the light of how she reacted to the different views of Ralph and Jack as the story developed. Although evaluation is a consideration of the novel as past experience, it is also one of the things a reader does in the midst of reading in order to make sense of what she reads.

We learn from experience and we learn from the representation of possible experience in fiction. Stories are not just amusements:

> We might be disposed to take stories more seriously if we perceived them
> first and foremost as a product of the human mind to narratize experience
> and to transform it into findings which as social beings we may share and
> compare with those of others.
>
> (Rosen, 1984, p. 12)

All readers make these findings, and go to stories on the look-out for
what they can observe of the rights and wrongs, the hows and whys of
human behaviour: they are especially important for young readers, who
are still mapping out where they stand in their treatment by others and
their treatment of others. Readers vary, of course, in their ability to make
explicit such interest, and to handle discourse about it. We have seen 8-
year-old Clayton trying to make clear what he has found in his reading
of *Watership Down*, in his letter to the author ('Why don't you call Bigwig
the Captain?') and his questioning of his teacher ('What would you trust
him for?'), both arising out of an uncertainty, in the midst of reading, as
to who is the leader. One of the things that Clayton learns is how to talk
about a story, and in the course of such conversation he also discovers
what there is to find in a story other than information. We are inclined to
think of such talk as the mark of more experienced readers, but their
experience lies more in their ability to formulate such responses than in
their need to discuss them.

What stories also make possible is the reader's involvement in impossible experience – shrinking children, flying snowmen, magic fingers,
talking rabbits, monster rats – as well as all those happenings that are
highly improbable, and unlikely ever to be part of the reader's life. We
play with such impossibilities outside our reading, too. Stories often
continue what has already begun in play, and they can also become the
material of games, and of our own story-telling.

The impossibility of a story confirms more positively our knowledge
that what we are reading *is* only a story; and the reassurance of that
makes possible the recognition, albeit unconscious, of other things that
are much closer to us. The further a story appears to be from us, the
more we are able to let it act secretly upon us over what most concerns
us.

All stories that most satisfy us act in this way. In this they are like
other playthings: there is a point in the Newsons' book about toys when
what is said could easily be as much about stories as about doll's houses:

> ... the miniature world ... gives [the child] the opportunity to experi-
> ment with actions, relationships, happenings and feelings at one remove
> from himself, to play with threatening ideas without being actively
> threatened, to try out a scenario of events without having to carry it
> through or take responsibility for the outcome, and in general to sort out

his ideas, both intellectual and emotive, on the safe play level. By the very
process of losing himself in this kind of play, he is enabled gradually to
find himself as a person.

(Newson and Newson, 1979, p. 124)

James Britton encouraged us to think of reading as a form of play, when
he drew our attention to the helpfulness of D. W. Winnicott's (1971)
concept of a 'third area':

> . . . an area of free activity lying between the world of shared and
> verifiable experience and the world of inner necessity . . .

(Britton, 1971, p. 43)

A story enables readers to enter that area, and through an act of
supposing to reconcile, or become reconciled to, tensions between the
world and their inner needs.

In *The Shrinking of Treehorn*, Treehorn is able to grow smaller or taller
by playing what Helen calls 'the game of life'; and stories offer similar
'games' to the imagination. Rachel was quite clear why she lost interest
in that book: it failed to match her own dream of staying small. But when
readers become lost in a story, they are unlikely, and unwilling, to be as
explicit as this: their activity as readers is multi-layered, and is in part the
working of a deep seam beyond the supervision of their consciousness.
Several times in this book I have attempted to bring to the surface some
of the subconscious response of these young readers: it is impossible to
be sure of the accuracy of these suppositions, but that is not to deny the
importance of the part the unconscious plays in a reader's response.

The Newsons write of finding oneself as a person through involvement in play, and, similarly, I want to think of reading as being a means
of seeing into ourselves. Stories offer a special kind of counsel and
comfort: readers find in them representations of their own unconscious
concerns – find without knowing what they have found, in stories that
do not know what they contain. It is a form of learning we know little
about – learning which we do not even conventionally term as such.

It may be possible to make some generalisations about the kinds of
psychological interest that fiction might hold for young readers. I
suggested, for example, that Enid Blyton's Secret Seven books were
attractive in that they satisfyingly combined 'adventure' with ordinary
homely routine; and I suspect that stories which, in a variety of
appearances, encourage feelings of independence – of being on your
own – but at the same time support feelings of dependency – of being
one of the family – are especially interesting to young readers. But we
cannot rely on such generalisations to describe individual responses,
which are frequently surprising and idiosyncratic: it would be a mistake,
even in the case of stories which seem universally popular, to make
predictions about any one reader's unconscious activity.

There are some books to which we become especially attached, and I have no doubt that what binds a reader to a book – in the first moment of choice, in the process of reading, in the keeping and treasuring of a book – is a movement of the unconscious towards the experience the book offers. Some children never make these special connections with stories, and have never learned to expect from their reading something akin to magic. Many of our schools still hold a narrow conception of what learning to read entails and of what there is to learn about reading, and still cling to the supposition that reading can be taught through activities and materials other than the encounter between child and genuine story. There lie in the unconscious of many children memories of early books that deter them in their future reading.

In their work with children and stories, teachers need to recognise the importance of the unconscious in shaping the responses of readers. We need to be patient with re-reading and re-telling, and to see these as the expression of a special interest in a story or part of a story. We need to provide, as Clayton's teacher did, time, and a variety of ways in which a child can give form to his reading experience, and further play with the imaginative material the story has provided. We must be prepared both for extensions and reversals of the story: sometimes an involvement with a story is expressed through work which seems a rejection of that story – which, for example, responds to the extraordinary with the ordinary, the magical with the mundane.

In this cherishing of response to books in children, teachers are doing their most delicate work, and their best.

Each time we read, we become more experienced as readers. Although some books resist us, and there are some we cannot see ourselves reading, each book we complete confirms us in our sense of ourselves as readers, and we acquire the confidence to look forward to new books and to reject those that are not to our liking. Sharon, the most experienced of these young readers, said before reading Lawrence for the first time, 'I want to find out what it's about . . . I'll be learning something new', and part of this learning pertains specifically to the development of her own reading practice.

Sharon said that beginning a book was to 'start from scratch' – 'you're learning all over again'. This is not altogether true, as we bring to each story our experience of reading previous stories, and our accumulated sense of what generally to expect from fiction. Karnail is obviously starting more from scratch in reading *Well Done, Secret Seven* than Sharon is in reading *Shardik*, and there will be ways in which Karnail starts less from scratch in reading *Good Work, Secret Seven* than Sharon reading *Sons and Lovers*. Our distance from scratch will vary for each one of us from book to book. For all readers, there are also times when what we begin to read so defies our expectations of a particular literary form that we are forced to return to base and rethink our approach. This can sometimes be too much for us. But our development as readers seems to be influenced by those times when we are made to reconsider our assumptions about the kind of story we find ourselves in, and how it asks to be read. We only notice ourselves reading when we are made to look, and these moments of recognition help us to grow further in our reading lives.

Each book we read asks us to follow its own 'language practice', sometimes requiring us to 'learn all over again', but at other times requiring us only to make minor adjustments to expectations we have already formed from previous stories. We have seen, for example, the varying kinds of difficulties Karnail has at the beginnings of a story; Philippa Pearce, at the start of *The Battle of Bubble and Squeak*, plays upon the experience of stories that she knows many of her young readers already possess, but Karnail is only puzzled by an opening which does not seem to him at all like the beginning of a story. For inexperienced readers, beginnings need to be inviting by being familiar, in keeping with their limited expectations of what stories will do (and we saw how Blyton made this, and everything else, much easier); but for more experienced readers, the invitation may be in the very unconventionality of the opening sentences. For all of us, however, there is a precariousness at the start of each new reading, because, in some part, we become beginners again.

Each story will present at least some of its readers with features that are new to them, however conventional its practice might seem to others. To give just three examaples: we saw that part of Hazel's problem with *Little House in the Big Woods* was the writer's practice of inserting Pa's stories into the main narrative, stories within the story; Joanne was puzzled by the convention of disaster novels whereby characters are introduced and made known to us, only to be abruptly disposed of; and Sharon, amongst other uncertainties, could not be sure whether she had identified the 'hero' or not. Perhaps it is possible to predict some of the difficulties for young readers, and so prepare and support them in their reading, or to encourage discussion of them in classroom conversations and through exchanges in reading journals. But such difficulties matter more or less to different readers at different times: often one of the reader's satisfactions is to overcome them on her own, as it was Sharon's; and always they are just one part of a complex of responses, which may override, or be overridden by, others in the decision whether to read on.

'It is clear,' writes Jonathan Culler in his chapter on literary competence, 'that study of one poem or novel facilitates the study of the next: one gains not only points of comparison but a sense of how to read' (Culler,

1975, p. 121). When we look back at our own reading careers, we can probably remember key texts, and trace how we have gradually become more competent as readers, still with some prejudices perhaps, but able to respond to a wide range of fictional practice. For none of us has this been a measured progress through a hierarchy of levels, or a career that has been carefully planned. Nor will it be for our children, or the children we teach. Children are their own best judges of what to read and when; growth in literary competence is a by-product of a process of consumption fuelled by more urgent personal needs. As adults, especially as teachers, we recommend books to children because they are just that bit more demanding, or compare interestingly with what has just been read, and that is often useful guidance; but more often than not, sooner or later, children will make their own new choices of books to read, frequently unpredictable and surprising. But it is important for young readers to know that there is an adult taking an especial interest in what they read, wanting to talk or write to them about that; and obviously it is crucially important that parents and teachers try to provide a wide variety of fiction from which to choose, so that children will find without going far to seek.

There are two elements in following a story which underlie competence in Culler's sense: picturing and remembering. I have already written in Sharon's chapter of picturing as a fundamental act of imagining by the reader necessary to making sense of what is read; and I suggested that a reader's various modes of picturing would be an important part of our characterisation of a reading process. In *Shardik*, locations are foreign to most readers' experience, and Sharon feels she has to make them more familiar by responding over-conscientiously to the detail in scenic depiction. For a less experienced reader, such as Karnail, this difficulty in picturing a scene can defeat the imagination. It is when there is little visual detail, and the scenes are close to home, as in Enid Blyton, that a reader can draw easily upon his own images of 'wood' or 'café' or 'fairground', without having to adjust to the text.

Most of the readers in this study need the support of some picturing external to their own imagining. We saw how closely Karnail 'read' the illustrations on book covers, and how easily he read *The Snowman*: the ease comes as much from the presence of the pictures as it does from the absence of the words. Helen's pleasure in re-reading her favourite books is also her pleasure in re-viewing their pictures: her response is to both illustration and text, read together. Hazel, on the other hand, is much more dismissive of illustrations, often deliberately ignoring them in order to discover the story for herself and let the words alone work on her imagination.

Clayton read *Watership Down*, having first studied the book of stills from the animated film: these help him in his own picturing of the story, which partly is externalised through his own drawings and his drama work. Joanne likes films that are versions of books she has read, not so much to help her in her reading at the time, but later to verify her own imaging of the story. Film and video are especially useful resources for teachers, but their images are so powerful that they can supplant what readers want to picture for themselves.

There are ways in which readers can be helped in their picturing at all ages: too often we leave older students to their own devices in their first reading of demanding set texts. There are also ways in which a reader's picturing can be a starting point for classroom activities. Certainly young readers can talk about the pictures they form as they read, both in general terms and in relation to individual books, and this is one of the ways in which they can become more aware of their own reading processes.

Clayton's illustrated book was also useful to him in being a reference point, an *aide-memoire* to the sequence of events in a very long story. Part of the satisfaction of a story is its completeness as experience, but part of a reader's difficulty is in holding the story in mind as it grows, remembering it sufficiently to appreciate its totality. It is especially difficult for young readers, who may not be able to read many pages at one time, and for whom length presents a real problem. Karnail talks about 'learning the story':

Karnail   . . . If I've read the first page / I'm on the second / I think of the first but keep up with the story.
DF   I'm not quite sure what you mean.
Karnail   If I've read the first page / um / I have to sort of learn the story / so I keep in my head what's the first page about and then read the second while I'm thinking / and go along from there.

The Secret Seven stories are full of reminders of where the story has reached: the text comes in manageable chunks, and is careful not to put too heavy a load upon the reader's memory. For the demands upon our memory, the pace at which we read or need to read, the decisions about what is significant and what is redundant, the need to predict as well as recollect – all these Karnail is inexperienced in, as he 'learns the story' page by page.

It has often been observed that the first response of young readers is to re-tell the story, not so much as a summary, but as a recollection. One of the reasons for this is the very real need to fix the story in the memory and to feel satisfyingly in command of the whole. We have to allow for this in classroom work, even though it sometimes strains the patience of a listener. There are activities, including forms of picturing, mapping and diagramming, which help children to keep hold of a long story in progress and to see something of its whole structure at the end: it is one aspect of a teacher's ingenuity to devise these freshly and appropriately for each novel read with a class.

Remembering the story as a whole is not the same as remembering the whole story, and this takes time to learn. But such remembering seems a crucial factor in the development of a reader's response. James Britton has written:

> As readers, we must first recreate the object in all its inner relatedness, and only then try to relate it as a whole to our own concerns, our own lives.
>
> (Britton, 1972, p. 176)

Young readers often dwell on certain parts of a story, forgetting much else; this is akin to the 'piecemeal contextualisation' that Britton describes as appropriate to reading non-fiction, although readers of fiction always remember, if only half-consciously, that their favourite bits are embedded in something complete and resolved. What we remember is governed as much by our unconscious responses as it is by our ability to memorise; but it is possible to 'learn the story' in the way that Britton describes, and thereby deepen our pleasure as we feel our own responses less fragmented and more satisfyingly whole.

At our most competent, we follow a text in order to play it, in the sense that Roland Barthes asks us to think of 'play':

> 'Playing' here must be understood in all its polysemy: the text itself plays (like a door, like a machine with 'play') and the reader plays twice over, playing the Text as one plays a game, looking for a practice which reproduces it, but, in order that that practice be not reduced to a passive inner mimesis (the Text is precisely that which resists such a reduction), also playing the Text in the musical sense of the term.
>
> (Barthes, 1977, p. 162)

Although structuralists and other literary theorists may want to construct a 'grammar' of fiction, a description of the system of conventions we draw upon in order to read stories, readers do not work from a set of explicit rules or preliminary instructions any more than do speakers. In that sense, reading is not a 'game'; but we read 'looking for a practice', the rules that apply in a particular reading, being able to do this because of our existing sense of possibilities and permutations derived from previous practice. At the same time, we play the text as we play a score, so that the experience of reading is one we create as much as receive. Reading is essentially interpretative, where interpretation is not the meaning we extract from a text, but what we take it to mean as we bring it into being.

We learn to follow the intricacies of the telling which make the story. Susanne Langer writes:

> . . . the whole fabric of illusory events takes its appearance and emotional value from the way the statements which actually compose the story are worded, the way the sentences flow, stop, repeat, stand alone, etc., the concentrations and expansions of statement, the charged or denuded words. The ways of telling make the place, the action, the characters in fiction . . .
>
> (Langer, 1953, p. 298)

The corollary of the ways of telling is the ways of reading, the movement of the reader's attention upon the words, the to and fro of the imagination as the fabric is woven.

When Sharon says 'I'll be learning something new', she speaks as a reader who is developing this kind of attentiveness and alertness. As she reads she learns, and what she learns is how to read this story: it is this learning which gives reading its fullest experiential feeling. We value fiction not because it is about experience, but because it *is* experience – in the 'virtual' sense that Susanne Langer has so helpfully explained (and which Sharon touched on in her final attempt to explain what reading is like). Our perceptions of ourselves as readers illuminate by analogy our perceptions of ourselves as learners, people who live through experiences and interpret them. 'It is as though,' writes Eagleton on behalf of Iser, 'what we have been "reading", in working our way through a book, is ourselves' (Eagleton, 1983, p. 79).

Here, then, is another sense in which we can help young people see themselves as readers. For if we can encourage children to talk about what happens as *they* read – and all the children in this study do that in their different ways – then they will grow into an awareness of themselves reading, which is another way of coming to understand how they learn, how they live, how they are.

The worst practice in schools does little to encourage the kinds of learning I have here associated with the experience of reading. I suspect that we attach little weight to those choices of fiction and responses to fiction that arise out of children's unconscious needs – for some time, during the conversations described here, I resisted and felt doubtful about their validity, although I now feel absolutely convinced of their importance. I want to think of stories as essential in the growing-up of children, and yet, as I write, we are authoritatively encouraged to make vocational objectives our priority. We still make the majority of our pupils take literature examinations, which for the most part lead to the teaching of fiction as received opinion rather than felt experience. Why do we value fiction? There are still people who foist books upon children as ways 'to help with your spelling' or 'improve your comprehension' or 'widen your vocabulary'.

Against this, there is the best practice, as demonstrated by the teachers and parents of the young people in this study. There has been, too, a general shift in literary studies to the activity of the reader from the performance of the writer, although it will take more than that for school examinations to give back reading to the young people reading. We especially need to insist that there are legitimate ways of writing about response other than the critical essay or the literary appreciation. Gabriel Josipovici wrote:

> . . . discourse about fiction is usually conducted in terms wholly in-adequate to our experience of it . . . it is very difficult to put into words *what happens* when we read a novel.
>
> (Josipovici, 1976, p. 10)

More recently, Terry Eagleton has said:

> Nobody is especially concerned about what you say, with what extreme, moderate, radical or conservative positions you adopt, provided that they are compatible with, and can be articulated within, a specific form of discourse.
>
> (Eagleton, 1983, p. 201)

In schools, perhaps we would do best to withdraw Literature as a core subject to be examined, and then to encourage reading, and the exploration of response in a range of written forms, through assignments for examination course work in Language.

Ian Gregor balances 'seeing a novel as a process evolving in time' with seeing a novel 'as a state contemplated spatially', and he asks:

> Are we not in danger of teaching all 'state' when our students are all 'process'?
>
> (Gregor, 1980, p. 193)

He writes:

> Arguably the more a critic seeks to *know* a text the less he exists as a reader . . . The 'normal' reader . . . will make his own unfinished text that is at once shifting, ambiguous, partial and *magical*. We should never 'know' the text, for the more we know and 'fix', the less we read.
>
> (ibid., p. 130)

These comments are encouraging to teachers in schools who are worried about the teaching of fiction: they urge us to attend to what happens in our students as they read; they stress those aspects of reading that cannot be explained and annotated, but which are magical. Their emphasis is upon young readers and their reading, as it happens, as it is experienced.

What I take from these conversations with Helen, Rachel, Clayton, Hazel, Karnail, Joanne and Sharon is something of that intent to preserve the real experience of reading: to be more alert to what fiction might mean in the lives of individual young readers; and to encourage, and make possible in the home and classroom, those activities which extend and prolong that experience through forms of play, acting out, and re-creation, and which deepen it through forms of talk and writing that give readers the chance to reflect upon their own processes, what happens as they read.

I want young people to see themselves as readers, in all senses of that phrase, and to see reading stories as a vital part of their experience of life.

Appendix A
The Snowman and Story-telling

When children tell the story of *The Snowman*, they reveal much of themselves as readers, even though the story has no words. As many of the children in Clayton's class enjoyed making a tape telling the story, it was possible to listen to a number of different versions.

The children tell the story in different ways.

1. The telling shows what the teller has valued in the story: different tellers place their emphases upon different elements – for example, the friendship between the boy and the snowman, or the fun of 'bossing' an adult, the fascination of the snowman himself (who is snowman/child/adult), and the sense of inevitable loss.

2. Some children read more in the detail of illustration than others, not only in what they closely observe and pick out, but in what they deduce from the drawn expressions of motivation and inner thought. In this way, the tellers reveal their sense of place and their understanding of character.

3. Some children add to what is already there, most obviously sounds, such as the creaking of the stairs, and what characters say. Their creation of dialogue between mother and son, for example, makes explicit the relationship between these characters and their behaviour towards each other.

4. The telling shows the child's sense of pace, shape and balance in the story. One child, for example, turns her story upon the line she gives her snowman: 'Now I'll show you my world.'

5. The telling also shows the teller's sense of an ending, and how the story inevitably moves towards it. Several children, for example, handle the detail of the electric fire and the gas stove with the clear sense of how these prefigure the eventual melting.

6. Different children use different narrative techniques in their choice of narrative voice and their use of dialogue, and also, more generally, in whether – to use Wayne Booth's distinction – they are tellers or showers.

110

7.   In the process of telling the story, the children reveal techniques
     common to all reading: scanning the page in front of them, looking
     ahead, adjusting and reshaping their telling as new information
     appears.

Apart from the value of this activity in itself, as a way for young readers
to re-create the story in their own version, it also enables the teacher to
make some useful observations of a child's reading, especially where
reading is taken to be not merely the articulation of words, but
approaches to books and ideas of story. It could be of more value to
teachers than conventional tests of reading – and, of course, more
enjoyable to the child.

Here is Karnail, in the first year of secondary school, telling his version
of *The Snowman*:

> This story is called *The Snowman*. There was a little boy who was about
> seven years old. He was asleep in bed and it was snowing outside and
> suddenly something happened and he opened his eyes and looked
> through the window. He cleaned the window and looked out hardly
> and / and he said it was snowing. He quickly got his jumper on and put his
> trousers on, and asked his mum if he could go out. So he got his
> wellingtons on, got his hat on, and ran outside . . .

Karnail was immediately interested in the book, and began to tell the
story of his own accord as he first turned the pages (although he made
this recording at a later date); but his telling seems less successful than
Clayton's (see Chapter 3). Clayton is more fluent, and has more verve;
he uses words more economically, and has a finer sense of pace. There
is some redundancy of detail in Karnail's version, and while he
conventionally establishes the narrative line Clayton propels us into the
story and makes the action live. On the other hand, Karnail in his phrase
'suddenly something happened' is trying to suggest the association
between the boy's waking and the coming of the snow; and whereas
Clayton's boy merely 'looked out', Karnail's cleans the window and
looks out 'hardly'.

   Both boys enjoyed telling the story, but Clayton, four years younger,
seems surer of his material and more resourceful: het gets hold of the
story and makes it his own. Both boys are 'beginning readers', but,
although Karnail may well read aloud more accurately and fluently, in
many ways he is a less accomplished reader than Clayton, as shown here
in the telling of *The Snowman*, and throughout the chapter about Clayton
and his reading of *Watership Down*.

Appendix B
The House of Wings:
A note on choosing
books

The House of Wings is by the American writer Betsy Byars. The front cover shows a three-storey wooden house, painted red and yellow, with seven windows, two in the roof, and a raised porch across the face of the house. There are geese on the porch, and there is a goose sitting on a window sill; upstairs another bird is sitting inside the room on the crossbar of the window frame. In front of the house there is long grass, in which there are more geese. In the foreground, walking towards the house, there are a boy and a man, both in overalls and check shirts. They are carrying a blue sack, from which protrude two long bird legs. The title is printed in white, superimposed upon the roof of the house; and the name of the author in light green at the top of the cover against a grey brown sky. On the back the house and the grass are continued; there are four and a half lines of small yellow print about the story.

Karnail picks up the book for the first time, holds it studying the picture on the front cover.

Karnail	This looks interesting.
DF	Now what made you say that?
Karnail	Because er / this / might be / a boy and his father / living in a / living on a farm.
DF	Yes.
Karnail	And / one day / someone might be / coming and killing their animals.
DF	What makes you say that? Oh there's something there you've seen is there?
Karnail	Yes.
DF	What / what's that do you think then?
Karnail	A sort a stork / looks like his legs.
DF	Yes it does a bit doesn't it, it's a bit difficult to see. What you think someone's come and killed that?
Karnail	Yeah and they'll have to bury it or something.

DF	And what is it that's interesting about that do you think? What do you think's going to happen?
Karnail	The way the house / has got / load of rooms for two.
DF	Yes. Yes it does seem a large house for just two people. What about the title?
Karnail	I can't see any wings!
DF	No it's a bit strange isn't it. Would that put you off or interest you?
Karnail	Put me off.

Hazel picks up the book for the first time.

Hazel	I don't know this what it means / these / live in the house / they live in a house / is that what the title means?
DF	Well it's
Hazel	Something like that?
DF	Of wings that
Hazel	The geese / living in the house
DF	Yes that's right
Hazel	They've got wings!
	. . .
DF	So what would you do? Would you say / Hm that doesn't make any sense / so I'll put it to one side or would you try and find out / a little more about it?
Hazel	I'd have a good look at it.

She opens the book in the middle, hesitantly because it is a new copy, and then turns back to the first page and reads. After a few seconds, she says 'I'd get that one'.

Sharon picks up the book, flicks through it: the shortness of the book, the size of the print, the cover – these suggest to her that it is a book for children. Is that why she rejects it so quickly? No, some children's books are good, although she prefers books that are longer. It is just that this is 'one of those books'; you can tell from the cover.

Sharon	You get these / books / and / it's just about families and what they do and / where they live in America and then the droughts all come and all their crops and it doesn't interest me.

Karnail relies entirely upon the picture for information about the book that he may or may not read: it could almost be said that he prefers to 'read' the picture than the book. Of the three, he is the one who scrutinises the picture most closely and, although he is wrong in his prediction of a likely event, he is right in other important details: that there are only two characters, that there is a 'stork' (crane), and that the house is oddly large. But he is deterred by his first glimpse of the *words* of the book: the title. It has a riddling quality, and he cannot match it to what he has observed in the picture.

When Karnail is beginning, Hazel is already practising, and the difference between the two can be seen in something as basic as the way they hold and handle the book. Hazel comes to the picture as a way of making sense of the title. It is the title that is her most important piece of information. (Only once did I see her consider at all closely the front-cover illustration of a book – *The Golden Bird*, with its silhouette pictures by Jan Pienkowski.) Although some titles are so strange that she turns away from the book immediately (for example, *How Many Miles to Babylon?* by Paula Fox), she usually makes use of other information in the book first. She is deliberate in this inspection, but has no set routine. Often she makes use of the Contents, but with *The House of Wings* she omitted this and sampled the text in the way that has been described. Although the title is puzzling, she accepts that it will be explained by the story and is happy for it to act in this retrospective way.

Sharon has much more experience of books, and knows the many different ways a book can give information about itself. She handles a book quickly and efficiently; it is as though she can 'feel' the book. What happens in this case is that her experience enables her to prejudge the book, in fact it prejudices her against it. Perhaps she resists the prejudice towards children's books – she claims that she does; but she mistakenly assigns the book to a category of story without giving it the chance to state its own nature. On the other hand, her categorisation is a sign of her experience as a reader.

Readers reject more books than they choose. There being so many books, no reader can be open to them all, and perhaps we need some prejudices in order to narrow the field. Sharon might one day read *The House of Wings*: one of the common experiences of a long-term reader is the pleasure of a book which was some time ago rejected.

Certainly there are ways of inspecting books and sampling them that young readers should learn about. In school, this is surely best done where they are free to handle many books in the company of other readers and a teacher. They can learn from watching and talking with each other; and teachers can help young readers by *telling* them about a book, by reading and talking to them during their own inspection of a book, and by prompting them as they handle the book in their presence.

But I suspect that this information more often confirms a reader in his choice than initiates it. What brings book and reader together is a sequence more complex and subjective than extracting information. When we meet a person, it helps to know something about him, but our first impressions depend as much upon appearance, personality, chance, whim, prejudice, what others have led us to believe, and so on. It may even be that what we seem to be doing is not what is registering in our minds. In much the same way, readers get on, or do not get on, with books.

Appendix C
A Note on Sharon's Books

Sharon made me a list of the books she has at home. Some of these are books she has bought herself:

1. *Watership Down*;
2. *The Plague Dogs*;
3. *The Grapes of Wrath*;
4. *Autobiography of Miss Jane Pittman*;
5. *Jane Eyre*;
6. *Shirley*;
7. *Mister Quilp* (abridged version of *Old Curiosity Shop*).
8. and some textbooks: biology, physics, home economics.

No. 4 she started, but gave up; no. 5 she has read twice, but has not read no. 6 yet; no. 7 she bought deliberately to help her with her reading of the Dickens book.

Other books are presents:

9. set of D. H. Lawrence novels;
10. *Roots*;
11. *Black Beauty*;
12. Bible.

Shardik was a present too. Several of her books were bought at junior school, either through the book club or at sales:

13. *In this House of Brede* (a story set in a convent);
14. *The Voyage of the Dawn Treader*;
15. *The Lion, the Witch and the Wardrobe*;
16. *Birds Beasts and Relatives*;
17. *A Zoo in my Luggage*;
18. *Children of the New Forest* ('a lot to read for a little bit to happen').

Nos. 14 and 15 she has read twice, and used to have the complete C. S. Lewis set. The Durrell books she read later, when she went to secondary school.

She has picked up several of her books at jumble sales:

19.   *The Red Pony*;
20.   *Jo's Boys*;
21.   *Mr Hudson's Diaries*;
22.   *American Heritage* (a textbook).

The other books in her list belong to other members of the family: they have either been given to Sharon or just strayed on to her shelves.

23.   *Old Curiosity Shop*;
24.   *Reading and Thinking*;
25.   *Jackals of the Sea* (Arthur Catherall).

No. 23 was her mother's (see no. 7); no. 24 belonged to her father when a boy; and no. 25 is her brother's, but she has not read it. She also has *Tom Sawyer*, but cannot remember where that came from.

Sharon was also able to tell me about books she remembered reading when she was younger. She is the only person in this study who has never read a book by Enid Blyton, but her list tells us that she did collect C. S. Lewis. She remembers, too, that she had a phase of reading stories about ballet and horses.

More recently, the Gerald Durrell books seem to have been important in the move from children's books into more adult reading: certainly Sharon feels they were. *Watership Down* has also been important to her. When I met her, the books she had read most recently and valued were the novels by Richard Adams, *Roots* by Alex Haley, and *Jane Eyre*.

There are other aspects of reading that Sharon is able to remember. For example: 'When I was young I used to be a bit embarrassed about looking at the adult books [in the library] because I thought I was too young . . . I didn't like to look at the adult books because I thought that people might think I was too young.' Comments such as this are useful not only in comprising a picture of this particular reader, but in alerting us to, and sometimes reminding us of feelings children have towards books and their provision.

It is not difficult for teachers to elicit this kind of information from their pupils; even something as simple as a list is revealing about a person as a reader, especially if there is time to go on to talk about the items on the list. Making lists is something most people enjoy doing. A list such as Sharon's seems much more informative than a grade or a reading age.

Appendix D
Extracts from the
Transcripts

First conversation with *Helen*, talking about *The Shrinking of Treehorn*, which she has read ten times

DF   Did you look at the back?

H   Yes. I saw his face was green.

DF   Yes. I'd missed that. I didn't see that. Whereas it wasn't on the front.

H   No, because, um, he gets smaller and then when it . . . at the end of it, he gets green. 'I won't tell anybody, I'll keep it to myself.'

DF   Why doesn't he tell anybody. Because it looks pretty awful, if you've got green . . . and his hands are green, too, now I look closely.

H   Because, um, what happened to him when he shrinked, everybody knew about it and kept fussing. So probably he doesn't want anybody to probably fuss about it when he turns green.

DF   When you say everybody, who is everybody in the story?

H   His mum and dad and the doctor and everything. He turns into the Incredible Hulk! *(giggles)*

DF   Well now, why don't you tell me a little bit about the story. You've got to remember I don't really know the story very well, because I only got the book the other day, and I just . . . well really I just flicked through it really.

H   *(chuckles)* Well he gets, he, er, . . . One day he wakes up and he finds he's getting smaller and smaller and he goes, and then, when he comes back from school, he keeps getting smaller and smaller. And then the next day he gets on the bus and the bus driver says, 'Wait, let this little boy get on.' And he says, 'Sit here by me if you want.' And so he settles down, and the bus driver kept saying, 'Are you Treehorn's brother?' And he said, 'No I'm Treehorn.' And the bus driver said, 'You must, er, that's a funny thing for naming two children called Treehorn.' And then when he gets home, in the morning, he plays a game its called a game of life, and he starts to grow again and he bumps his head on the bed, and then, and then the next day after that he gets . . . er . . . his mum, his mum's friends are coming and he turns, and he . . . and his mum comes in and says

117

'Brush your hair' and he looks in the mirror and he's turned green.

DF What was this bit about the game?

H   He plays a game and he landed on a square and, er, it said go six places forward, and so he went six places forward and, um, he started to grow again to his normal size. And he bumped his head on the bed.

DF What's the game called?

H   Um, a game of life, I think.

DF So what are you saying? Is that the reason he gets smaller and larger?

H   Mmm.

DF Now, what you said earlier, that all these people were making a fuss about him when they found out that he was shrinking.

H   Mmm, because they, they probably didn't know anybody would shrink, and they probably would make a fuss and everything.

DF Well they were worried.

H   Mmm.

DF What about Treehorn himself? If I woke up in the morning and found myself getting smaller . . .

H   He weren't really bothered. His mum didn't take any notice of him. She was in the kitchen and when he came down the first morning when he was shrinking, he tripped over his trousers, and his mummy said, 'Please watch what you're doing, you're going to ruin my cake,' because she's got a cake in the oven and she's not wondering about what he's saying to her, 'cos he's saying, 'My trousers are getting too long, my sleeves are getting too long', and she's saying, 'Be quiet, this cake won't turn out right.' That's all she's saying to him.

DF So she's more worried about the cake than . . .

H   Yes, more worried about the cake than him.

DF So she's not, I mean, she's not really fussing then, is she? She's not worried either.

H   No. And then, that night, she's really fussing about it.

DF Oh I see.

H   She says call a doctor or something to the father. 'He is really shrinking now. What shall we do?'

DF What about dad? Is dad worried?

H   Yes. And it says in . . . I'll go and look in the yellow pages.

DF Find a doctor who can cure shrinking. And do they find a doctor?

H   No. He goes to school, and goes to the water fountain and he can't reach it, and the teacher comes along and he's jumping up and down trying to get some water and she said, 'Stop that Treehorn! Just because you're shrinking it doesn't mean you can jump up and down to get some water out of the water fountain. If everybody did that the whole school would fall down.' And then when he went home, um, he went to bed and in the morning he played the game, and he started getting bigger and bigger and then the next day he turned green. And that was the end of the story, and the mother goes into the kitchen.

DF   And do they worry about him being green? Or do they . . .

H   No.

DF   It stops there does it?

H   It stops there.

DF   What do you think they'll do about him being green?

H   Same as they done to when he was shrinking. 'Cos, he went to the doctor in the school, and he went in and then the doctor said, he gave him a form, the doctor didn't do nothing, he said 'If you need me, come and I'll do anything for you' and he hadn't done anything for him, and he just walked out, and he hadn't done anything for him so it wasn't worth seeing him.

DF   No.

H   And then he went home and then he wrote a letter 'cos he always gets these things from cereal boxes and he sent it off and he couldn't reach, um, the letterbox so his friend put it in for him.

DF   What, because he was so small?

H   Yes, and the letterbox was about (?) foot high. And then when he goes home he has his dinner, his mum's always worrying about him. Ever so funny. And then it stops at the end of the book.

First conversation with Clayton, discussing *The Snowman*

C   This part where he ate some ice cubes. And this is my second favourite one. Now he's in the in the fridge in the garage. That's the second one I like. And there's um that one I like because I think he ate the food cold and he ate his hot I think . . .
     . . . I like that bit where he runs and flies takes off. And this is my favourite, the sad part, when he melts at the end.

DF   Yes. Yes it is a bit sad isn't it.

C   Yes. Usually when I when I do it I don't look at the end page.

DF   Why?

C   It's so sad.

DF   What when you read this book you don't look at the last page?

C   No. I always turn it over to the white, to the white pages and then go back to the front cover (. . .?).

DF   Even though you know what's on the page?

C   Yes.

DF   I took it down as a present to a little boy of a friend of mine in Wales and he's only three and a half and he got to the last page I thought he was going to cry, because he was a bit sad about it.

C   Did he?

DF   No, he sort of said he said Oooh, he sort of groaned like that you know. He sounded really upset.
     Did you know it was going to happen?

C   Er, no, not when I first looked at it.

DF   What did you think, how did you think it would end?

C   When he's in bed. Then he goes, then he comes from, um, Frosty (?) and he sleeps in bed, and that's where it ends. That's what I thought (. . .) I didn't look, I didn't like that piece.

DF   Do you think the book would have been better without that page? Would you sooner have the book without that?

C   No.

DF   So

C   Would be sillier.

DF   So if that was just a blank page there . . .

C   He could make another one!

Second conversation with Hazel, discussing *Little House in the Big Woods*

DF   Tell me a bit more about the father. Is he the sort of main character in the story?

H   *[7 seconds]* I don't know.

DF   What sort of a father is he? Can you tell me a little bit about him as he is in the book?

H   What, what do you mean, what like?

DF   Well, um, is he, is he in the book very much the father?

H   Yeah.

DF   So he's there quite a lot of the time. All right. How does he behave towards his children and towards his mother. Do they see much of him?

H   Yeah, except for when he goes out hunting.

DF   What kind of a man is he. I mean, is he, um, is he a good man?

H   *[8 seconds]* Um.

DF   Has he done anything that's bad or silly?

H   No.

DF   So he's a sensible man and they can rely on him, can they? Um, how about the children is he strict with them?

H   On Sundays he is.

DF   Why?

H   He doesn't let them run about and play . . . He just reads the Bible to them and that's all they do.

DF   It doesn't sound very exciting Sunday.

H   No. And he used to tell them story about his, the grandad, and, he used to, his, one story said that, there, um, they were reading a catechism whatever it is, yeah I had to do that when I got confirmed . . .

H   I've just read the, um, bit about (pause), um, they go to the grandpa's further down in the wood and he makes sugar, sugar, small sugar cakes. He gets, um, he puts, he makes a hole in trees and puts a bucket underneath and every day he comes to collect what comes out of the trees, and he gets, he makes a big, um, bonfire and has a big pot and he puts it on, he gets two chains each side and hangs them from the tree and keeps stirring it.

DF   And this if he gets it just right makes sugar does it?

H   Yeah he lets it cool and it makes sugar. And then that night there's a ball and that's all that I've read to.

DF   In the story there seem to be quite a lot of bits like that about people making things and doing things . . . Do you find those bits more interesting or less interesting than the other kinds of bits where she's sort of telling stories about narrow escapes with the bear . . .

H   The best bits I like is when, um, the father tells the stories about his travels going to town and trading his things and about his grandad when he was small . . .

Last Conversation with Karnail

DF   Does it sort of stay in here or do you forget it pretty quickly?

K   No it stays in there for a time.

DF   In what sort of way is it in there? Do you, you don't, do you find yourself thinking about it?

K   Yes. 'Cos if it's a good book with adventures in it, it stays in there.

DF   What, what stays there?

K   The best parts so far, like, the best part, it stays in the head.

DF   Does it stay in the head as a kind of memory, or as a picture, or what?

K   A sort of memory, I think.

DF   Like when you think about things that you've actually done yourself in the past. Is it like that?

K   Yes.

DF   Mmm. Is it very clear. I mean, can you remember exactly what happened?

K   No, I forget half of it.

DF   It's sort of there?

K   Yes.

DF   What about as you're actually reading a story. What's in there as you're reading a story?

K   Mmm. What I've read. If I've read the first page, I'm on the second, I think of the first but keep up with the story.

DF   I'm not quite sure what you mean.

K   If I've read the first page, um, I have to sort of learn the story, so I keep in my head what's the first page about and then read the second while I'm thinking, and go along from there.

DF   So you're sort of, um, as you go further into the book, what's in your head is a memory, remembering what you've already read. Are you, so you're looking back as it were. Do you look forward at all? Do you are you sort of thinking about what might happen?

K   No.

DF   Do you sort of see the story, as it were, do you sort of see it coming to life like you were watching a film?

K   Yes. Yes, sometimes I do when it's a really good story. Keep on thinking about what the children might be doing.

DF   What, you sort of see it do you?
K   Yes.
DF   When you see it, is it as though you're watching a film or is it not quite like that?
K   Not quite like that, because I'm not really seeing it just thinking of it in my mind.
DF   Do you sort of see yourself in the story or
K   No. Just the people who are in it.
DF   Sometimes you see people in school for example and there's a whole room full of children at break and there's some people reading and they don't seem to notice all the noise at all.
K   Think they're in a dream world.
DF   Yes, in a dream world yes. Now is it a bit like that do you think?
K   Yeah, because you forget everything about what's going on, and just read the book.
DF   Mmm. Now you said, you know you said earlier about, um, sort of seeing it in your head, is that like a dream?
K   I don't know. *[9 seconds]* Sort of like a dream. Say that, if I'm reading a book and that could happen tomorrow. Like that.
DF   How is that like a dream?
K   Say if I'm dreaming of getting a bike tomorrow.
DF   Oh I see, yes, yes. And as you're reading a story it could actually come true . . . It could come true as it were?
K   Yes.
DF   What, to you or to them?
K   To me!

Second conversation with Joanne, discussing *The Rats*

J   They are things that could really happen to you, and the way the author explains them, as if he has really had the experience . . .
      . . . I suppose I love children and the one part was a little baby sitting on the kitchen floor, and, um, the mother's making a cup of tea, this is in London, in London, and they've all got cellars in London, in these houses, everybody, everything that's happened to different people who have been killed they've all got cellars, and all the schools have got cellars, so everywhere has got cellars. And, um, this mother is making a cup of tea and she hasn't got any tea, she realises she hasn't got any tea, she's boiled the kettle and etcetera and she hasn't got any tea and she really wants a cup of tea so she looks at the baby and she says 'Oh I'll just pop next door and, er, get some tea'. So, the author makes you realise that she has only gone for two minutes but in those two minutes the door of the cellar was slightly open and the one rat, they called them rodents in the [. . .?] creatures, comes in to the kitchen out of the cellar and sits and stares at the baby and the baby's just a baby and she's sitting there playing with this puppy, you see, um, and the rat, first of all it bites at the, because the little baby is moving its fingers, bit the fingers and

that made it snatch away, and the puppy is trying to, um, fight this rat off 'cause it's hurting the baby and he can see what's happening so then the rat turns to the puppy and then more of the rats come in when they've smelt the blood, more of the rats come in so, um, there's more and more coming in and the baby is, um, sort of torn apart, it's arm is eaten chopped off, sounds horrid doesn't it, and, um, then the mother comes back, that's two minutes and then the mother comes back and she sees them and she runs in chonking on all these rats and they seem to ignore the mother till it picks up the baby out of them eating, it's covered in blood, she picks up the baby and she runs out but her legs have been, you know, sort of scraped and scratched and she shuts the front door and that's it. She just runs and runs until she gets to this police station. And earlier on in the book we, I found out that, um, one scratch or bite kills them in 24 hours, kills them in 24 hours . . .

. . . So the mother died and the baby did of course, 'cause she was dead anyway, and that's it. That was just one part. We never heard anything about them again, that was just it, they died.

. . .

There's been one man, Mr Harris his name is, who, er, Harris, no not Mr Harris, who has been, um, in the story all the way through, he's been the police's link and now he's the biochemist's link and the ratkiller's link etc. etc. and, er, because he's had experiences with the, with the rats and he's never been hurt there's always somebody who's never hurt but been close to it and has never been bitten . . .

. . . but again Harris was always saved. He came into contact with them all the time he'd always got a crowbar or something which he hurled, (held?), just about to jump on him and land on this crowbar and it would always miss him but it was so close to him and everybody else got, I mean the headmaster was killed . . .

DF   Is Harris the hero?
J   Yes I think so.
DF   He's still in the book is he?
J   Yes he's still in the book. I think he will be until the end. I mean there was, right at the beginning, there was the ratkiller man, the head of the whole lot, and he was . . . kneeling down . . . and one of the rats came out and bit his face out.

Conversation with Sharon and Joanne

S   Perhaps it's, um, I mean, it's just, when you're reading a book, you're not actually in like 1979 sitting in your bedroom you're in with the story itself in some other world. Not actually, but in your mind you are.
J   I found that when I was reading *London Morning*.
DF   Go on.

J   You can, um, imagine being in London and the school she went to and the things that went on in the school.

DF   Yes.

J   Going back, in that time.

DF   Yes. When you say you can imagine it, and you can, what was your phrase, you can imagine yourself . . .?

S   In some, in a world of, the book is in your mind, you can imagine that you're somewhere else.

DF   Yes. Can we just get at that a little bit more precisely, and see if you're both saying the same thing. Are you, are you simply saying that you can picture it?

S   No. You can actually *feel* that you're there. Um, I'm, I'm trying to think of something I can use as an example. *[6 second pause]* Like with, um, the first scene in *Jane Eyre* where she's sitting in the window seat with the rain outside, you can actually feel the cold window panes and the rain beating against them, and how lonely she is, you know. You really feel sorry for her, feel it yourself, I mean, you imagine yourself being there, being a little girl sitting in the window seat.

DF   You actually imagine yourself as the character?

S   Yes.

DF   In the story. Or you imagine yourself being there and looking at the character?

S   No, as the character herself.

DF   Actually as the character herself. What about when you read *London Morning*, did you actually feel, did you actually sort of make yourself feel as though you were the character, the girl in *London Morning*?

J   *[pause]* No, I was somebody watching her doing what she was doing, you know, doing, the actual things that she did.

DF   Yes. When you say watching her, sorry about all these questions flying at you.

J   That's all right!

DF   When you say watching her, um, do you mean watching her like you would watch say, um, a film, or do you mean.

J   No, you're walking behind her, standing right behind her, wat . . . doing the things she does.

DF   So it's as though you're actually in the story?

J   Yes.

S   But you don't see yourself there.

J   No no. You don't see yourself there, You're like a shadow. No you can't see.

DF   What to yourself or the characters?

J   To yourself.

DF   Yes. And you're watching. Is that what, that's slightly different from what you're saying isn't it?

S   Yes. I'm saying that I actually feel that I am the person.

J   In all the books that you read?

DF   Just what I was going to say.

S   Well, it depends, depends on the book. I mean,

J   When I read, oh are you watching, um, read Oliver, *Oliver Twist*, you can go back to then, you can imagine those times?

S   In certain parts in some books you can imagine you're the person but in others you're *with* them but not actually them themselves. Like, um, in *The Plague Dogs* in some parts you can actually feel you're the dog, seeing and everything he sees and looking where he does but then at other times you're beside him looking at the dog himself.

DF   Yes. Would you say that was your experience that it does depend

J   Yes.

DF   On the book and also on what's happening in the book at that particular time. So you're sort of sometimes you are very close like a very close watcher but at other times you're so close you're almost the character herself, or himself, or itself, if it's a dog.

J   It depends what, it really does depend though on the, on the book that you're reading.

Last Conversation with Sharon

DF   When you're reading a book like that, is it almost as though you're sort of living at that time, you're living in that world?

S   Yes it's like as if you're there but they can't see you and you can just see them.

DF   But presumably you're doing more than just watching are you?

S   Oh, yes, I mean, you feel what they feel, and you, you only see what they see, you know, you can't go off.

DF   And are you, do you think you're making, yes you're feeling, are you also . . . What kind of thinking are you doing. I mean, are you saying to yourself, are you sort of trying to make decisions about whether people have behaved badly or not or why they've behaved the way they have?

S   What, do you mean, while you're reading?

DF   Mmm, yes, while you're reading and also sort of between reads as it were or after the read's over. I think you're going to say aren't you that as you're actually reading the text you're not actually thinking that?

S   As, as you read it you just read what's there but sometimes you can think Oh well she could have done this, you know, this would have been all right you know, she, um, she could have run away but she stayed there, you know, you think of things she could have done but she hasn't, you know, you have to follow the book. I find myself thinking that sometimes, you know, when in between reading but not while I'm reading.
       . . .

DF   . . . Do you think books, books even if they're not, even if they're not obviously like life as you know it, they still in a way reflect upon life as you know it or might know it, the fact that by reading them you come to know life, understand things like, you know, what you said before, seeing the other side.

S   Yes I think you do. *[10 second pause]* Can't think of how to explain . . . it's like, um, experiencing something but you haven't actually lived through it *[6 second pause]* I don't think I connect, you know, connect them with my life, myself. I might do it subconsciously but I don't think Oh I do that or I do something like that.

DF   No. I'm sure you're right when you say it is a kind of experiencing.

S   Yes.

DF   And that thing you said last time, I don't know whether you've thought about it again since, but that when you start a book you, you start under way, it's like learning from scratch . . .

S   Yes. 'Cos I've got a set of books I had for Christmas at home and I'm dying to get started on them, 'cos at the moment I've got no idea what they're about and then, whatsoever, I know I'm going to start on *Sons and Lovers*, 'cos I've planned it all out! When I've finished my exams I'm going to finish *Shardik* and then read that. You know, I'm dying to get on to it but I know that I've got my revision to do. And it's just, it's, you know, I want to find out what it's about, and I'll just pick it up and read the first line and after I read a few pages I'll know a bit more and then a few more and I'll know a bit more and, you know, by the time I get into the book I will know the characters and that, I'll be learning something new.

DF   And if that works really well that's why you feel strange at the end because in a way you become so familiar with the world of that book and with, almost as though you know the people in the book, and suddenly you've lost them.

S   It's like a death really isn't it? You've lost them and you can't really get in touch again.

DF   Yes, it is like a death, but that's, if the book's your own, you can always sort of

S   Yes.

DF   resurrect it.

S   But, er, perhaps that's like, like memories and photographs (. . .)

DF   But it's not quite the same is it when you read a book the second time?

S   No, it's never, never the same again.

DF   Are there times do you think when that kind of learning is too difficult?

S   What's that?

DF   Well, that, you know, that you pick it up and the book is just too strange, just can't make it familiar . . .

S   Yes, there are some books like that. I tried to read one of Gerald Durrell, is it, I tried to read one of his books once. I've read some quite a while ago, I remember trying to read one but, you know, I just couldn't get into it. I just couldn't relate to the, you know, to what was happening in the book. I couldn't imagine it myself.

DF   Relate to what was happening. Now . . .

S   By that I mean I couldn't sort of um piece the pieces together you know and make it into something that I, you know, something that, um, was individual to me, how I saw the book, I couldn't make that for myself.

References

Applebee, A. (1977). The elements of response to a literary work: What we have learned. *Research in Teaching English*, II(3), Winter.

(1978). *The Child's Concept of Story*. Chicago, University of Chicago Press.

Barthes, R. (1977). *Image–Music–Text*. London, Fontana.

Benjamin, W. (1977). *Illuminations*. London, Fontana.

Benton, M. (ed.) (1980). *Approaches to Research in Children's Literature*. University of Southampton.

Bettelheim, B. (1978). *The Uses of Enchantment*. Harmondsworth, Penguin.

Britton, J. (1971) The role of fantasy. *English in Education*, Winter Sheffield, NATE.

(1972). *Language and Learning*. Harmondsworth, Penguin.

Clark, M. (1976). *Young Fluent Readers*. London, Heinemann Educational Books.

Craig, G. (1976). Reading: who is doing what to whom? In G. Josipovici (ed.), *The Modern English Novel*. London, Open Books.

Culler, J. (1975). *Structuralist Poetics*. London, Routledge & Kegan Paul.

Eagleton, T. (1983). *Literary Theory*. Oxford, Basil Blackwell.

Gregor, I. (ed.) (1980). *Reading the Victorian Novel: Detail into Form*. London, Vision Press.

Harding, D. W. (1962). *Psychological Processes in the reading of fiction*. British Journal of Aesthetics Vol. 2 No. 2.

(1967) *Considered Experience: The Invitation of the Novel. English in Education*. Sheffield, NATE.

Irwin, M. (1979). *Picturing*. London, Routledge & Kegan Paul.

Iser, W. (1978). *The Act of Reading*. London, Routledge & Kegan Paul.

Josipovici, G. (ed.) (1976). *The Modern English Novel*. London, Open Books.

Langer, S. (1953). *Feeling and Form*. London, Routledge & Kegan Paul.

Morris, R. (1973). *Success and Failure in Learning to Read*. Harmondsworth, Penguin.

Newson, J. and Newson, E. (1979). *Toys and Playthings*. Harmondsworth, Penguin.

Perkins, V. F. (1972). *Film as Film*. Harmondsworth, Penguin.

Rosen, H. (1984). *Stories and Meanings*. Sheffield, NATE.

Rosenblatt, L. M. (1970). *Literature as Exploration*. London, Heinemann Educational Books.

Smith, F. (1973). *Psycholinguistics and Reading*. New York, Holt, Rinehart & Winston.

Steiner, G. (1978). *On Difficulty and Other Essays*. Oxford, Oxford University Press.

Stevens, W. (1953). The house was quiet and the world was calm. In *Selected Poems*. London, Faber.

Tucker, N. (1981). *The Child and the Book*. Cambridge, Cambridge University Press.

Whitehead, F. (1977). *Children and their Books*. London, Macmillan.

Winnicott, D. W. (1971). *Playing and Reality*. Harmondsworth, Penguin.

Fiction mentioned in the text

Richard Adams, *Watership Down*, Penguin
Richard Adams, *Shardik*, Penguin
Valerie Avery, *London Morning*, Arnold–Wheaton
Enid Blyton, *Secret Seven series*, Knight
Raymond Briggs, *The Snowman*, Hamish Hamilton
Edith Brill, *The Golden Bird*, Puffin
Charlotte Brontë, *Jane Eyre*, Penguin
Betsy Byars, *The House of Wings*, Puffin
Roald Dahl, *The Magic Finger*, Puffin
Paula Fox, *How Many Miles to Babylon?*, Puffin
William Golding, *Lord of the Flies*, Faber
F. Parry Heide, *Shrinking of Treehorn*, Puffin
James Herbert, *The Rats*, New English Library
D. H. Lawrence, *Sons and Lovers*, Penguin
Robert Leeson, *The Demon Bike Rider*, Armada
Jan Mark, *Thunder and Lightnings*, Puffin
James Vance Marshall, *Walkabout*, Puffin
Charles May, *Stranger in the Storm*, Grasshopper Abelard
Richard Parker, *Snatched*, Puffin
Philippa Pearce, *The Battle of Bubble and Squeak*, Puffin
Beatrix Potter, *Pigling Bland*, Warne
Laura Ingalls Wilder, *Little House in the Big Woods*, Puffin

Index

131